UNDERSTANDING YOUR BIBLE

UNDERSTANDING YOUR BIBLE

An Introduction to Dispensationalism

S. Craig MacDonald

Grace Gospel Fellowship

Grace Gospel Fellowship
Grand Rapids, Michigan 49509

Understanding Your Bible

ISBN 0-89814-027-7

Printed in the United States of America
Second Printing, February 2002

te deum

Contents

Preface .... *ix*

1 • Hermeneutics 1
"I can read what it says, but what does it mean?"

2 • Oikonomia 13
A special word, a special application

3 • Identifying the Dispensations 22
Gaining an overview of God's work in history

4 • Nailing Down the Start 44
Locating the beginning point for this dispensation

5 • What Must I Do To Be Saved?............... 60
Salvation in dispensationalism

6 • Looking to the Future 75
Different dispensations, different futures

7 • We Do Not Want You To Be Ignorant 96
God's plan for the Body of Christ

8 • Miracles in Dispensationalism 108
"Is God still doing them?"

9 • Water Baptism.................................... 125
Sorting out teaching and tradition

10 • The Transition Period 146
A unique time in history

11 • Dispensationalism as a System 164
A look at the whole

PREFACE

For most of us the word *primer* brings to mind the gray paint auto body shops use before they spray on the color coat. But in my grandparents' time the word was pronounced as though it were spelled *primmer* and it had a completely different meaning. In those days a primer was a book of basics, of elementary principles. Usually the word was associated with a book designed to teach children to read, although it was also used for any book which taught the beginning principles of a subject.

This book is a primer, and it is very important you understand this before you begin reading. The aim on the following pages is to introduce you to dispensational theology. For some readers the topic may be so new they are not even sure how to pronounce the word. Others may be quite familiar with this area of theology and capable of teaching it to others. The latter group should understand this book is written for the former group.

Because this is a primer it does not do a lot of things it otherwise should. It does not quote extensively from other books and journal articles. Beginners are sometimes frustrated when they have to sort through what a whole group of people is saying about a particular point. They just want to know the basics, not every angle on the topic. In fact, this book does not even have long lists of supporting Scripture references. It seeks to quote just enough verses to show that the position taken is biblical or to illustrate the point being made.

You also will not read an elaborate defense of the views presented in this book. In a more advanced study of dispensationalism it would be appropriate to anticipate any objections which someone might have and respond to them. Very little of that will be found here. In a few cases it will help the reader understand the dispensational position if it is contrasted with other views. But for the most part the following pages will just state the position, not try to defend it against any challenge.

This approach runs the risk that the absence of a defense will be interpreted to mean none exists. But as soon as a book tries to eliminate that risk by anticipating and answering objections it stops being a primer and starts becoming something much more complex than the beginner needs. Every journey into a new area of knowledge starts somewhere, and most of us find it easiest to start with the basics.

Hopefully, this little primer will whet your appetite for more. Perhaps you will even have objections as you read. Good! We should all be like the residents of Berea who listened to Paul and "examined the Scriptures every day to see if what Paul said was true" (Acts 17:11). Like the gray paint the auto body shop uses, this book is meant to be a base which will lead to more study. Books and articles are available which will take you to the next level and beyond. Most importantly, the goal of this book is to encourage you to read your Bible, because there is where the truth resides. Never let this or any other book take the place only God's Word should have.

- Chapter 1 -

HERMENEUTICS

"I can read what it says, but what does it mean?"

Do you remember your high school English teacher asking what the author really meant when he wrote the story or poem you had just read? That question frustrated me. Why not let the piece mean just what it said? Why did there always have to be some deeper meaning?

My English teacher (her name was Mrs. Mally) was working from a different perspective. As it turns out, I think I agree with her now. She understood Herman Melville was not just writing an interesting story about a ship captain chasing a big white whale. The novel *Moby Dick* tells us about the great struggles which go on inside each of us. And *The Count of Monte Cristo* by Alexandre Dumas is more than a story about escape and revenge. It is a discussion of how life often pays us back according to our actions. Many times a piece of literature has a deeper and more significant message than the literal meaning of the words. To miss this more important message is to miss the real purpose of the work.

The careful study of what a particular piece of literature means and how it should be understood is called *hermeneutics*, from a Greek word meaning interpretation. Basically two hermeneutical options exist. The first option understands words to mean no more and no less than what they say. That is, a particular piece of literature is taken at face value and interpreted literally without any secondary or deeper symbolic meaning. Most of what we read falls into this category. The newspaper, your favorite magazine, and letters you get in the mail are examples. If my Aunt Josephine writes that she went to the circus last week, I don't wonder what she *really* means. I assume she did in fact go to the circus.

The other option is to view literature as having deeper symbolical meanings, which are the real message the author wants to get across. Aunt Josephine may not have gone to the circus at all. What she may mean to tell me is that life last week was full of one wild and crazy event after another. In this case, if I restrict myself to a literal reading I miss the most important point of her letter.

When doing Bible study the issue of hermeneutics is very important. Once you have decided the Bible is indeed the Word of God and without error, you have to decide which method of interpretation is appropriate, the literal or the symbolic. Is the Bible to be understood as meaning essentially what it says? Or are the words of Scripture meant to be interpreted allegorically in order to teach us truths deeper and more significant than may appear on the surface? Here Protestant evangelicals disagree. While they agree most of the Bible can and should be taken literally, some take certain passages, especially those containing promises and prophecies, as allegories to be fulfilled not in a literal sense but spiritually within the lives of believers. Others advocate a more completely literal approach and take words and phrases throughout Scripture at face value. Using this method, prophecies which promise dramatic events in the future are interpreted literally no matter how startling it may seem.

EXERCISING OUR OPTIONS

Perhaps a good example of these two hermeneutical options at work is Isaiah 11. In verses 6 and 7 Isaiah says that in the future there will be peace in the animal kingdom. The wolf will live with the lamb, the cow will feed with the bear, and the lion will eat straw like the ox. Interpreted literally, we understand these verses to say that God will at some point in the future restore the animals to a condition of peace like that which existed in the Garden of Eden. When you stop to think about the implications of such an action, including the necessary changes in their digestive systems, this would certainly be a remarkable development!

However, using a nonliteral, or allegorical hermeneutic leads to a very different interpretation of this passage. Then Isaiah would not be telling us meat eating animals will be changed to vegetarians. According to the nonliteralist this kind of rigid literalism misses the point and makes the passage say something God did not intend. Rather, God is telling us that at some point in the future (at least from Isaiah's perspective) God will restore peace on earth. Since Scripture is not primarily concerned with the animal creation but with man and his spiritual condition, the use of animals here is a metaphor, a figure of speech. The prophet merely uses animals to figuratively represent the peace and harmony which will exist on earth when the gospel changes the hearts of humankind.

It should be said at this point that it is possible for people on either side of this issue to be genuinely saved. The passages we are considering here are not those which deal with Christ's substitutionary death or our salvation by faith apart from works. These passages do not have to do with our salvation. Rather, they have to do with God's plan for humanity and what He is doing and will do for His people. So it is important to keep these matters in perspective.

It should be every Christian's goal to better understand the Bible and all it teaches about God's plan for humankind throughout history. But the most important truth in Scripture is that all individuals may come to salvation through Jesus Christ. No truth of Scripture is more plain or more significant than that concerning the work of Christ on our behalf and the role of faith in accepting God's gift of salvation. Those of us who have accepted Christ as our personal Savior are united as brothers and sisters in Christ, and no disagreement should be stronger than that bond. Whether we use a literal or a figurative hermeneutic will significantly affect how we understand God's plan throughout human history and our obedience to God's will. Some of the issues which will be discussed in this book are central to how we live the Christian life and they deserve careful study. But they must be kept secondary to the doctrine of salvation.

MAKING A CHOICE

In his book *Dispensationalism Today*, Charles Ryrie gives three convincing reasons why a literal method is the better hermeneutical principle. First, God is the One who created mankind and gave us the ability to communicate. Certainly, a major factor in this aspect of creation was God's desire to communicate with us. A wise God would create language in a way adequate to fulfill its purpose in normal usage. It simply does not make sense that God would desire to communicate with us, yet create language in such a way that it requires some special sense to accomplish its task. Taking words at their face value is the more appropriate way to accomplish His purpose.

To illustrate, suppose I wanted to invent a device which would help me get from my home to a city 100 miles away. I spend hours out in the garage and produce a vehicle with four wheels, including two in front for steering. My vehicle also has a motor connected to the wheels providing adequate power, and seats for myself and any passengers I want to take along. After all this is done I roll it out of the garage, load up my passengers, and begin pushing the vehicle from behind. Every few yards I run up to the front and reposition the wheels to guide the vehicle in the right direction, and then return to pushing.

This scenario is ridiculous. If my goal is to create a vehicle to transport me to my destination I should make it adequate to perform its function and then use it in its normal manner. In the same way, if God wanted to communicate with us He would create language adequate to the task and then use it in its normal manner. The literal understanding of language is normal; an allegorical method is a specialized usage.

Using our Isaiah 11 text again, if God did in fact want to tell us there would be dramatic changes in the animal kingdom, how could He do it apart from using words in their normal, or literal way? To understand the passage literally is certainly the most natural approach. Ryrie calls this reason for a literal hermeneutic the "philosophical argument" because it is based on the purpose of language.

A second reason Ryrie gives for literal interpretation is the "biblical argument." One of the things the Bible student notices about prophecies concerning the first coming of Jesus Christ is that they were all fulfilled literally. He was born of a virgin (Isa. 7:14) in the city of Bethlehem (Micah 5:2) exactly as the prophets predicted. The very words of Psalm 22 were spoken by Christ on the cross, and He was assigned a grave with the wicked and with the rich, just as the prophet said (Isa. 53:9). Since the prophecies about His first coming were all fulfilled literally there is no reason to think the prophecies concerning His future plans should be understood any differently. The Bible student should expect all the promises of Scripture which are yet to come to pass to be fulfilled in precisely the same way all those regarding His first advent were fulfilled—literally.

Thirdly, a "logical reason" can be given for using a literal hermeneutic. If the passage does not mean what it says but instead has some deeper, figurative meaning, who determines what that meaning is? Suddenly no objectivity is left in Bible study. Using an allegorical hermeneutic our interpretations of a given passage would be very different, but there is no sure way to identify which, if any of us, is correct. When Isaiah says that at a future time the wolf will live with the lamb, and that is not to be understood literally, who determines exactly what the metaphor *does* mean? Is it a reference to personal peace, or social peace, or political peace? Zechariah 14:4 says the Lord will stand on the Mount of Olives and deliver Israel from her enemies. If this reference to a geographical point on earth does not really mean the Mount of Olives, and if this is not really about the nation of Israel but about something else, who decides what that something else is? Why is my interpretation any better than yours? Only by taking words and phrases at their face value is there any objectivity and any confidence in understanding the Bible.

Once we have adopted a literal hermeneutic, the work is only beginning. Everyone agrees that even in everyday conversation when we intend to be taken literally, we still use figures of speech. I may say, "I am so hungry I could eat a cow," but I certainly do not want you to set a Hereford in front of me, nor do I have to explain myself. In our language and culture this expression is understood as hyperbole, or exaggeration for the sake of emphasis.

Figures of speech have been used in all cultures and in every age. For this reason many have said that in this context a better term than "literal" interpretation is "normal" or "plain" interpretation. These terms recognize legitimate figures of speech in Scripture. But how does one decide which phrase is a figure of speech and how it should be understood? The answer is by careful and thorough study. Archeology has been a big help here, as has the work done by scholars in the biblical languages. Together they identify phrases which in the cultures of biblical times were commonly understood to mean something other than what they literally say.

The key is to determine what a given word or group of words normally meant to readers living at that time. A technical Latin term for this, *usus loquendi*, means the use of words in their cultural location. So the question is, did the average person in Isaiah's day, for example, understand our passage in chapter 11 to be a common figure of speech, or did he take it literally?

As it turns out, the Bible has very few passages which are open to question in this area. For the most part, we know enough about the languages and cultures represented in the Bible to determine which phrases were understood by the original readers as figures of speech. However, some specific passages are still debated even by those who use a literal, or normal hermeneutic. Perhaps the best example of this would be those sections of the book of Revelation which discuss the battles to be fought at the end of human history. Will those battles be fought with literal swords and from literal horses, or are those terms figures of speech used to represent weapons at a time when guns and tanks were unknown? Respected interpreters disagree. But all those committed to a literal or normal hermeneutic do agree there will be real battles fought at some point in the future between real armies. It is not just a figurative reference to the internal struggles of the Christian life.

Thus, your hermeneutics determine to a large extent how you understand the Bible. If, when you come to certain passages, you adopt a figurative interpretation, you will understand God's plan and program in a very different way than if you take a literal or normal approach. As we have seen, only the literal or normal method of interpretation is fully adequate for properly understanding Scripture.

WHEN WE USE A LITERAL HERMENEUTIC

One of the most significant results of using a literal hermeneutic is the distinction between Israel and the Body of Christ. Since the term Israel, when used in the historical sections of the Old Testament, clearly means the people who descended from Jacob, the literalist understands the term to mean the same thing throughout Scripture. That is, unless the writer of a particular passage clearly indicates he means the term to be understood in some special, "non-normal" sense we should take it just as his original readers undoubtedly understood it, namely as a reference to the physical nation.

This nation of Israel was the focal point of God's work in the Old Testament. In Exodus 19:5,6, God tells them, "If you obey me fully and keep my covenant, then out of all nations you will be my treasured possession. Although the whole earth is mine, you will be for me a kingdom of priests and a holy nation." The apostle Paul illustrates the special status of the people of Israel when he points out, "Theirs is the adoption as sons; theirs the divine glory, the covenants, the receiving of the law, the temple worship and the promises. Theirs are the patriarchs, and from them is traced the human ancestry of Christ, who is God over all, forever praised! Amen" (Rom. 9:4,5). God gave Israel a land, established the Davidic kingdom, and promised that the kingdom would endure forever (2 Sam. 7:16).

In contrast to the term *Israel* stands the phrase *Body of Christ*. The apostle Paul describes the Body of Christ as being distinctly nonphysical, not associated with a particular national or ethnic group, nor tied to a particular land. In Galatians 3:28, Paul says to believers, "There is neither Jew nor Greek, slave nor free, male nor female, for you are all one in Christ Jesus." In Ephesians 2:13, Paul speaks to Gentiles and tells them, "Now in Christ Jesus you who once were far away have been brought near through the blood of Christ." In Romans 10:12 he writes, "For there is no difference between Jew and Gentile—the same Lord is Lord of all and richly blesses all who call on him." Those statements, and others like them, clearly show a contrast between the nation of Israel and the Body of Christ where no ethnic or national distinctions exist.

The Bible student who comes to Scripture with a nonliteral, or allegorical method of interpretation sees the Body of Christ as a new, spiritual form of Old Testament Israel. He believes the promises made to the nation of Israel were never meant to be fulfilled literally but are brought to pass figuratively and spiritually through the Church and members of the Body of Christ.

In contrast, the Bible student who uses a literal hermeneutic cannot blend these two entities, Israel and the Body of Christ, and somehow make them synonymous. The Body of Christ is not the current Israel existing in spiritual or figurative form. It is separate and distinct. The blessings promised to Israel remain uniquely hers, and any which have not yet been fulfilled (there are many!) will be brought to pass literally at some point in the future.

CONCLUSION

The matter of hermeneutics is very important to Bible study. If your method of interpretation views the Bible as using symbolism and figurative language as a basic method of communication, you will view the Body of Christ as the spiritualized form of Israel. In the outgrowth of God's program, then, the physical nation of Israel has become the spiritual Body of Christ. Promises made to Israel about the future should thus be interpreted as metaphors to describe the spiritual blessings which come to Christians in this day and age. On the other hand, if you use a literal or normal hermeneutic you will understand the Body of Christ to be separate and distinct from the nation Israel, not just its current form. Any promises made to Israel which have not already been fulfilled are still hers and await future fulfillment. The terms *Israel* and *Body of Christ* cannot in any sense be understood as synonyms.

Because of the reasons given earlier in this chapter, we believe the literal method of interpretation is the only hermeneutic which does justice to the Scriptures. As a result, we view the Body of Christ as different from the nation Israel, not an extension of it. This raises interesting questions about how the change from one program to the other took place. How is it God could apparently stop His dealings with Israel and begin the Body of Christ? Such a view also implies that in the future God will renew His special relationship with Israel in order to fulfill the promises He made to her. The Bible is not silent on these matters, and our next chapter will explore this area.

STUDY QUESTIONS

1. What does the word *hermeneutics* mean?
2. What are the two hermeneutical options?
3. Why is the term *normal* better than *literal*?
4. Of the two hermeneutical options, which is the better? Give the three reasons for your answer.
5. What is one of the most significant results of choosing this option?

- Chapter 2 -

OIKONOMIA

A special word, a special application

Words are fascinating. Some are interesting because of their origins, or etymology. The hippopotamus gets its name from Greek words meaning river horse. Other words have very peculiar meanings, like cleave, which means both to cling together and to divide. Some terms represent not just a simple thing or action but a complex set of concepts. For example, the word democracy implies a number of underlying ideas in association with each other. It suggests a governmental relationship where supreme power rests with the people and is exercised through a system of free elections. A word like democracy represents a concept which requires a longer and more descriptive definition.

The Greek language had big "concept" words, too. One of those was *oikonomia* from which we get our word economy. In chapter 1 we noted that it is important to determine the *usus loquendi* of biblical words and phrases. What did they mean to the original readers? Fortunately, we have an excellent guide to the meaning of *oikonomia* in Luke 16 where Christ tells His disciples a parable. In this passage the word "management" is the English translation of *oikonomia* and the word "manager" is the translation of the related word *oikonomos*.

> Jesus told his disciples: "There was a rich man whose manager was accused of wasting his possessions. So he called him in and asked him, 'What is this I hear about you? Give an account of your management, because you cannot be manager any longer.'
>
> "The manager said to himself, 'What shall I do now? My master is taking away my job. I'm not strong enough to dig, and I'm ashamed to beg—I know what I'll do so that, when I lose my job here, people will welcome me into their houses'" (Luke 16:1-4).

The parable goes on to tell of the manager's plan to save himself from financial ruin and the practical lesson to be learned from his behavior. But, because parables were taken from the situations of everyday life, Christ here gives a clear picture of the *usus loquendi* of the word *oikonomia*.

The first basic feature of an *oikonomia* is that it includes two individuals or parties, in this case a rich man and the manager who is called the *oikonomos*. These two individuals have a vertical relationship. That is, the rich man holds a position of authority over the manager or steward of his estate. In our culture we normally think of a manager as being a superior who has people under him. But in this context the manager, or *oikonomos*, is the subordinate who is under the authority of the owner.

Secondly, specific responsibilities are assigned to the manager by the one over him. In the parable, the manager was to oversee the rich man's possessions. Thirdly, the manager may be called upon at any time to give an account of his stewardship, to see if he has fulfilled all his responsibilities. Finally, if the manager has failed in any way, it is the option of his superior to dismiss him. The superior is not obliged to dismiss the manager but can if he wants to. In that event, the superior may want to bring in another manager.

These four features of an *oikonomia* can be illustrated with the following diagram. Notice we have substituted the term "Party #1" for the rich man and "Party #2" for the manager. This will help us in future discussions. The break in the line between the boxes represents Party #1's option of ending the *oikonomia* if the manager or *oikonomos* fails to carry out his responsibilities.

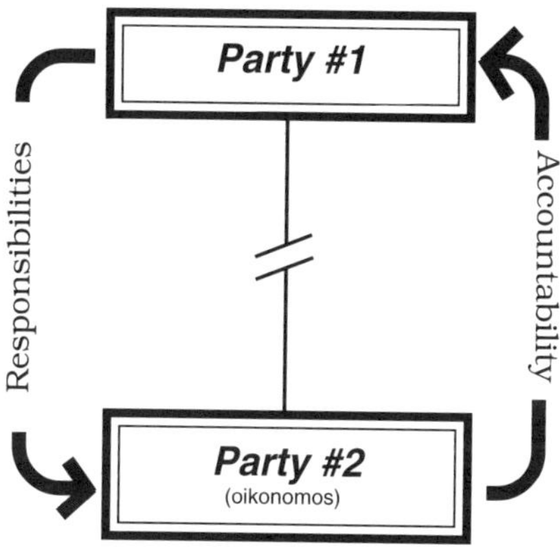

Figure 2.a

If the manager or *oikonomos* does not carry out his responsibilities and is therefore replaced with a new one, Party #1 will have to communicate to this new manager his specific responsibilities. This may involve three possibilities. First, some of the duties of the previous manager may be carried over into this new relationship. Secondly, some of the previous obligations may be discontinued, so that the new *oikonomos* is no longer responsible for them. Thirdly, new duties may be added. But whatever the combination of responsibilities given to the new manager, he too will be held accountable for his performance and liable to replacement should he prove unfaithful in the performance of his duties.

This economic system of rich men and managers was a very normal part of culture during New Testament times and was as familiar to them as the free enterprise system is to us. Perhaps the closest thing to an *oikonomos* in our day is the ranch foreman who has management over the cattle ranch owned by his wealthy boss. The boss may have assigned him responsibility for all aspects of the cattle business from feeding to marketing. However, if the boss calls the foreman into his office and learns the operation has been poorly managed, he may either graciously give the foreman another chance or fire him and hire another foreman. With the hiring of a new foreman the responsibilities may be changed. This new man may continue to be in charge of raising the cattle but no longer be responsible for marketing them. In addition, he may be given responsibility for managing a new herd of horses the rancher wants to buy. In other words, there will be some combination of continued, discontinued, and new responsibilities. Of course, the rancher will have to call the new foreman into the office to communicate to him the specifics of his stewardship. Without such a discussion the new foreman would have no idea what his specific responsibilities were. This scenario is probably closer to the television image of a wealthy rancher than it is to real life, but it serves to illustrate the basic features of an *oikonomia*.

What makes the concept of an *oikonomia* so significant is that the Bible uses the term to describe how God has been dealing with humankind throughout the course of human history. In Ephesians 1:10, the New American Standard Version translated *oikonomia* with the word "administration": ". . . with a view to an *administration* suitable to the fullness of the times, that is, the summing up of all things in Christ, things in the heavens and things upon the earth." The King James Version translates *oikonomia* in this verse with the word "dispensation," from the Latin word for dispense. But more important than the English word used is a proper understanding of the original meaning. Here Paul uses the concept of an *oikonomia* to characterize God's relationship with humankind at a time still in the future.

In Ephesians 3, Paul again uses *oikonomia*, this time to describe the present situation. In verse 2 he writes, "Surely you have heard about the administration [*oikonomia*] of God's grace that was given to me for you." In verse 9, we read of the ministry God gave Paul when he says, ". . . and to make plain to everyone the administration [*oikonomia*] of this mystery, which for ages past was kept hidden in God, who created all things." When the Christians in the Ephesian church read those words they readily brought to mind all the basic features of an *oikonomia* outlined above. They understood Paul to be saying God is dealing with humankind in the same way and with the same dynamics which characterize an *oikonomia*. God as Party #1 has given humankind specific responsibilities, held humankind accountable, and when it was appropriate, made changes in the *oikonomos*.

It is important to note that Paul uses the term *oikonomia* in its everyday sense. He also indicates God has had at least three separate administrations or dispensations: the one which preceded the *oikonomia* revealed to Paul, the present one, and the administration which is yet future. As we shall see, a careful study of the Bible indicates there have been more than three, but each one will have the four aspects of a normal *oikonomia* discussed above. God will be Party #1 in each, and humankind or a portion of humankind will be Party #2. One or more specific responsibilities will be given and, sadly, Party #2 will consistently fail to measure up. Most of the time God in His grace does not exercise His option to end the *oikonomia*. However, in each one there comes a time when God calls Party #2 to account, and changes in the *oikonomos* are made.

When a change is made, the expected pattern is followed. God exercises His sovereign will in selecting a new manager, or Party #2, and the combination of continuing, deleted, and new responsibilities are laid out. This requires that the new steward (or a representative if the stewardship is being given to a group) be "called into the office" and told the terms of the new *oikonomia*. Because we are now dealing with a relationship between God and man, this communication takes the form of divine revelation. That is, God supernaturally communicates His will with regard to the new management or dispensation through direct communication.

Notice that in Ephesians 3:2 Paul said, "The administration [*oikonomia*] of God's grace that was given *to* me *for* you." Paul understood himself to be the receiver of the revelation of the new terms and conditions for this dispensation.

At this point we can take what we have learned and get a picture of what the Bible says about God's dealings with humankind over the course of history. God has administered a series of *oikonomias*, each with different stewards (Party #2), and with varying responsibilities. The fact that there have been several *oikonomias* is due to humankind's failure to fulfill the responsibilities assigned him in each of them.

Because the King James Version generally translated *oikonomia* with the word "dispensation," this became the most common designation for these relationships. Whether we use the word dispensation or management or stewardship is not as important as understanding the concepts involved. However, because dispensation has become the standard term in the literature on the subject, it is the one we will use for our discussion. Dispensationalism, then, refers to the form of theology which recognizes several separate *oikonomias* in Scripture, and a dispensationalist is one who holds to that theology.

PUTTING IT ALL TOGETHER

It is interesting to note how well a dispensational understanding of Scripture fits with the need for literal interpretation which we discussed in chapter one. At the close of the chapter we asked how God could stop His dealings with Israel and begin the Body of Christ. The answer is through a change in dispensations. When God makes promises about the future which involve dramatic changes in the way all creation lives, we do not need to turn these into metaphors without any clear or certain meaning. They simply describe a dispensation with standards and conditions different from our current one. The contradictions which some people see in the Bible are not contradictions at all and do not need to be explained away with imaginative interpretations. Rather, in different dispensations God has given different principles to be obeyed. Thus, in one dispensation humans can eat anything and in another only "clean" animals are allowable. The rite of circumcision may be required at one time and absolutely unnecessary at another. God may deal specially and exclusively with Israel and then set Israel aside to bring in a new Party #2 where national origin is of no value.

A literal hermeneutic results in a dispensational understanding of Scripture, and dispensationalism is consistent with a literal hermeneutic, the only one which does justice to the words of Scripture. The other option is to interpret Scripture figuratively and understand God as working one continuous uniform program. This approach, known as covenant theology, comes in different forms, but to a greater or lesser extent covenant theology views the kinds of changes in God's dealings discussed above as not being changes at all, but rather different metaphors to describe the same spiritual truths. This makes the interpretation of Scripture too subjective and does not fit with the fact that all the prophecies about Christ's first coming were fulfilled very literally. Only a literal hermeneutic and a dispensational approach do justice to Scripture. Certainly some truths and aspects of God's relationship with humankind remain constant and unchanged. There is unity in the way God has dealt with us, but not uniformity.

Once the Bible student has settled on a literal hermeneutic and its result, namely dispensationalism, another question presents itself. How many of these *oikonomias* are in the Bible, and what are their respective features? This is where we go next.

STUDY QUESTIONS

1. What are the four concepts in the word *oikonomia*?
2. What combination of three things may happen when a new manager is brought in?
3. Name one of the passages where Paul uses the word *oikonomia* to describe God's dealings with humankind.
4. What has become the standard English word for expressing the concepts of the word *oikonomia*?
5. What form of theology uses a more figurative hermeneutic?

- *Chapter 3* -

IDENTIFYING THE DISPENSATIONS

Gaining an overview of God's work in history

The apostle Paul writing under the inspiration of the Holy Spirit chose the term *oikonomia* to describe God's dealings with humankind through history. Charles Ryrie in his book *Dispensationalism Today* gives a helpful definition of an *oikonomia* or dispensation by describing it as, "a distinguishable economy in the outworking of God's purpose." In other words, God has a purpose, a plan He is carrying out, and He has dealt with different individuals or groups (Party #2) in different ways as He directs this plan through the course of history.

These distinct economies are recognizable as we read through the Bible. Therefore, it becomes an important part of good Bible study to identify these dispensations and the characteristics of each. As Christians we want to know God, and one way to do this is to understand how He has worked with people in the past. We also want to know what He desires from us now. If the specific responsibilities vary from dispensation to dispensation, we need to recognize those distinctions so we do not misapply instructions from another dispensation to our situation. What foods should we be eating, and what ceremonies should be part of our worship? These and other important questions can only be answered by correctly understanding the dispensational dimension of God's plan.

It might be wise to remind ourselves here that not everything changes with a new dispensation. Remember, when there is a change in an *oikonomia* some instructions will be added, some removed, and others will continue. Occasionally people get concerned that dispensationalism will result in "throwing out" all of the Bible except those portions specifically written to this current dispensation, because all other sections are considered irrelevant. The apostle Paul said "All Scripture is God-breathed and is useful . . ." (2 Tim. 3:16). Studying the portions of Scripture written to those in other dispensations brings at least two significant benefits. First, those portions tell us something about the Person and work of God. We learn of His attributes and nature as we see Him deal with humankind in any age. Secondly, much of what God commands carries over through succeeding dispensations. Murder is wrong when Cain kills Abel, when David has Uriah killed, and when Paul denounces it in Romans 13:9. Much insight is available to the Christian who carefully reads the Old Testament for guidelines on very contemporary matters like profanity, lust, and social justice.

A SERIES OF DISPENSATIONS

One way to visualize the combination of continuing and withdrawn commands is to depict history as a time line. This line is made up of segments, each representing a period of time during which God was administering a particular dispensation. Those commands intended by God to apply only to one particular dispensation are *vertical* and those which apply to succeeding dispensations are *horizontal*. For example, the command not to eat of the tree of the knowledge of good and evil would be vertical, pertaining only to the dispensation which governed God's dealings with humankind during the period in the Garden of Eden. The prohibition against taking another human's life is an horizontal truth, applying to Cain and all succeeding dispensations.

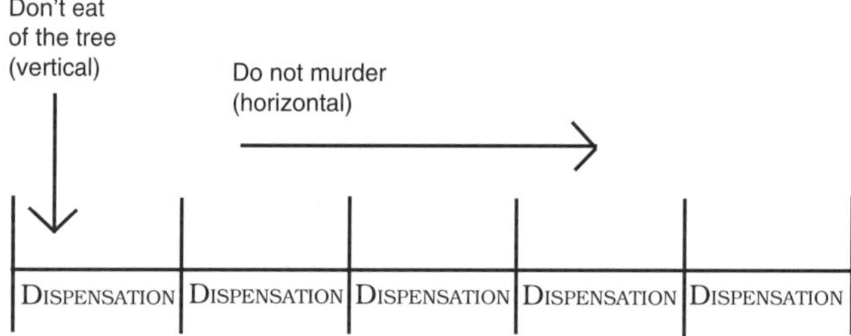

Figure 3.a

Understanding, then, the importance of recognizing the dispensational aspect of God's dealings with humankind, how can we discover what dispensations have occurred or will occur and when they begin and end? Because God will be Party #1 in every *oikonomia*, the best way to identify the separate dispensations is to look for major changes in the other features of the relationship. Does God seem to have changed the person or group with whom He is dealing (Party #2)? Are new and significantly different instructions given which govern humankind's relationship with God and others?

The term "test" is sometimes used to describe the unique set of specific responsibilities given to Party #2 in each dispensation and the term "failure" is used to describe the inevitable results of humankind's efforts. As we read through the Bible we should expect to see a "judgment" or severing of the relationship just before any dispensational change, and the change should include the revelation necessary to communicate the directives for the new *oikonomia*.

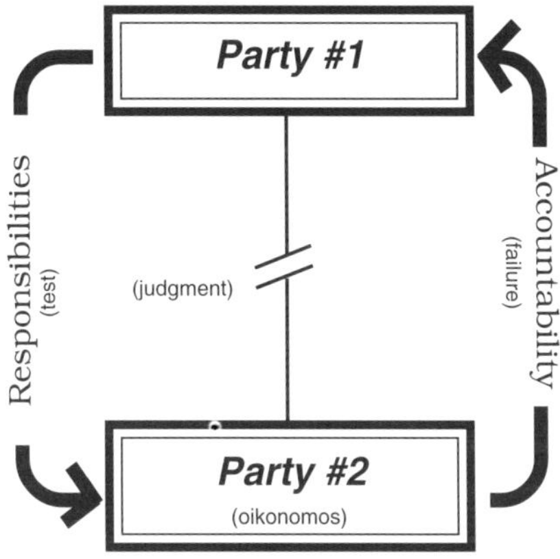

Figure 3.b

Applying this test, failure, judgment pattern to the flow of history as revealed in Scripture serves as an effective way to identify the various dispensations and their respective Party #2. However, while

Scripture teaches that God has worked through a series of *oikonomias*, the Bible is not primarily a systematic record of those dispensations. If that were the main purpose of Scripture we would find a very complete accounting of all features of each dispensation. Instead, we find them clearly presented in some cases and implied in others. The fact that the biblical information on some dispensations is not as clear as it is for others does not invalidate the dispensational approach to Scripture. Remember, the apostle Paul uses the word *oikonomia* to describe God's dealings with humankind. This tells us the approach is not only valid, it is biblical. But in some cases the features of a particular *oikonomia* will be more clear than others.

The first distinguishable *oikonomia* in Scripture is the relationship God had with Adam and Eve in the Garden of Eden. God is Party #1, and in this case the stewards, or Party #2, are obviously Adam and Eve. The test, or set of specific responsibilities, is also clearly laid out. They were to both fill and subdue the earth (Gen. 1:28) and to avoid eating from the tree of the knowledge of good and evil (Gen. 2:15-17). As we know, they failed the test when both of them ate the fruit of that tree. Note that it is not necessary to fall short in every detail of the test; failure in any one of the responsibilities makes the steward subject to being removed. And so in Genesis 3:16-19 God dispenses judgment on Adam and Eve and their descendants. Women will endure pain in childbirth, men will experience painful toil as they work, and death will be the destiny of all. As Adam and Eve are expelled from the Garden, the first dispensation comes to an end.

It is relatively easy to decide which of the instructions given to Adam and Eve as Party #2 are vertical, that is, are no longer in effect as the next dispensation begins. No one since Genesis 3 has had opportunity to eat or not eat of the forbidden tree. However, the question as to whether or not the instruction to fill and subdue the earth is still in force is an interesting one indeed. If it is a horizontal command, when should we consider it accomplished? Is there a point at which we begin to overpopulate or oppress the earth?

This first dispensation has traditionally been called the dispensation of Innocence because up until the time they ate the forbidden fruit Adam and Eve were morally innocent of any sin. But, as Paul tells us in Romans 5, Adam's failure brought sad consequences on them and on all of us as their descendants. Another abiding result of that first sin was the result suggested by the name of the tree, the tree of the knowledge of good and evil. Humankind now possesses the experiential knowledge of good and evil; humankind has a conscience.

Though no direct statement is made about the test in the second dispensation and no record is given of the revelation which communicated it, it seems clear each individual was held accountable to respond to his/her conscience and avoid that which he/she instinctively knew to be evil. But humankind failed this test almost immediately as Cain killed his brother Abel, an action which, as his later defensiveness proves, he knew was wrong. God could have ended this second *oikonomia* at that point, but He dealt graciously with Cain and with those who followed. By the time we get to Genesis

6:5 we read, "The LORD saw how great man's wickedness on the earth had become, and that every inclination of the thoughts of his heart was only evil all the time." After a pattern of failing to respond to his/her conscience, humankind had deteriorated to the extent that God pronounced judgment. "So the LORD said, 'I will wipe humankind, whom I have created, from the face of the earth—men and animals, and creatures that move along the ground, and birds of the air—for I am grieved that I have made them'" (Gen. 6:7). In the next chapters we read of the flood which God used as the means of judgment on humankind, sparing only Noah and his family, thus ending the dispensation.

This second *oikonomia* has traditionally been labeled the dispensation of Conscience, taken from the test or specific responsibility which was given. Again we can ask if the command to obey our conscience is horizontal and operative today. In 1 Timothy 4:2 Paul talks about teachers "whose consciences have been seared as with a hot iron." This would seem to indicate our consciences may not be an appropriate guide for behavior, and to follow one's conscience may lead to serious error. Perhaps in the early stages of human history sin had not so thoroughly permeated humankind, and the conscience was a more effective guide. However, the conscience may serve even today as a partial aid to proper conduct. The fact that these teachers had seared consciences indicates they do not receive from their consciences the direction they should.

After only two dispensations we see the test, failure, judgment pattern which characterizes the change from one *oikonomia* to the next. We can also see the combination of discontinued, continuing, and new responsibilities given as the dispensations change. In the first dispensation, Innocence, Adam and Eve were Party #2, and in the second dispensation, Conscience, all of humankind was Party #2.

It is helpful to keep a chart of our study as we identify the various dispensations and their features. Our observations so far would look like this:

Name	Innocence	Conscience	
Test	Fill, Subdue, Don't Eat	Obey Conscience	
Failure	Ate	EVIL!	
Judgment	Cast out, Pain & Toil, Death	Flood	
Party #2	Adam & Eve	Humankind	

Figure 3.c

After the judgment of the flood, God began a new *oikonomia* by speaking to Noah (revelation) and giving him the particular responsibilities he and his descendants were to carry out. Again, humankind is Party #2. The specifics of the test begin in Genesis 9:1 where we read the first instruction: "Then God blessed Noah and his sons, saying to them, 'Be fruitful and increase in number and fill the earth.'" God goes on to tell Noah that humanity's diet has now been expanded to include all living things. Until now humankind has been vegetarian (see Gen. 1:29). But from this point, "Everything that lives and moves will be food for you. Just as I gave you the green plants, I now give you everything" (Gen. 9:3). Also, whereas before this God Himself administered justice on those guilty of murder, this responsibility now is assigned to society. "Whoever sheds the blood of man, by man shall his blood be shed; for in the image of God has God made man" (Gen. 9:6). It is this last instruction which provides the name traditionally given to this dispensation, Human Government. It has been said the ultimate expression of the power of the state is the use of capital punishment, and because God here assigns this responsibility to humankind, the designation Human Government has been used. If it were up to us, we might give this dispensation a name which did not focus on just one feature of the test, but the name Human Government has been used for so long it has become the standard designation.

How did humankind do at fulfilling the new responsibilities? We need only turn a few pages to read that humanity again failed the test. Genesis 11 records the attempt to build the tower at Babel. The account opens with the explanatory statement describing one aspect of the culture of the day: "... the whole world had one language and a common speech" (v. 1). In verse 4, their goal in building the tower is given. "Then they said, 'Come, let us build ourselves a city, with a tower that reaches to the heavens, so that we may make a name for ourselves and not be scattered over the face of the whole earth.'" Many of us have assumed the sin here was the sin of pride in attempting to build a tower which would reach up to God. But the phrase "a tower that reaches to the heavens" merely describes one which will be very tall. Their sinful goal was to provide a structure which would serve as a focal point for their culture and prevent the very scattering over the earth which God had commanded.

This failure is followed by God's judgment. First, He did forcefully that which they refused to do voluntarily; He scattered them over the face of the earth. He also confused their language so that they could no longer communicate effectively with each other. The creation of different languages had the effect of preventing this kind of unanimous rebellion against the command of God from happening again, but it also served as a continuing judgment on humankind. It is still felt today as our missionaries struggle through language barriers in presenting the gospel. And how much of the suspicion and hostility between peoples today comes as a result of our inability to understand what the other is saying?

Name	Innocence	Conscience	Human Gov't	
Test	Fill, Subdue, Don't Eat	Obey Conscience	Fill and Subdue	
Failure	Ate	EVIL!	Gathering at Babel	
Judgment	Cast out, Pain & Toil, Death	Flood	Confusion of Languages	
Party #2	Adam & Eve	Humankind	Humankind	

Figure 3.d

This test, failure, judgment pattern has now been repeated three times. In each case, Party #2 has been all of humankind, although in the first dispensation humankind was only Adam and Eve. This pattern changes dramatically as we move to the next dispensation. In Genesis 12:1, God calls Abram to leave his country and his people and go to live in a new land. This clear test is followed with the promise that God will make Abram, later renamed Abraham, and his descendants into a great nation. Furthermore, God will treat all other people in the same manner they treat Abraham's people. Those who bless Abram and his descendants will, in turn, be blessed by God, but those who curse them will be cursed by God (Gen. 12:3). We know from the New Testament that God is here beginning the process of selecting the line through which Christ will come, as well as raising up the nation Israel.

The rest of the book of Genesis is fascinating reading as we follow Abraham and his offspring through one adventure after another. But, how did they do at obeying the part of the test which commanded them to stay in the Promised Land? Before we are even out of chapter 12, Abraham has gone down to Egypt to avoid a famine in the land. Despite telling a dangerous lie about Sarah being his sister, God graciously brings him back to the land appointed for him.

In Genesis 26, we read of another famine, this time during the days of Isaac, Abraham's son. In verse 2 we read, "The Lord appeared to Isaac and said, 'Do not go down to Egypt; live in the land where I tell you to live.'" To his credit, Isaac was in this respect more faithful than his father and remained in the land.

Beginning in chapter 37, we have the account of Joseph, son of Jacob, son of Isaac. Joseph was sold into slavery by his brothers and ended up in Egypt. After an extraordinary series of events clearly guided by God, he ended up serving as Pharaoh's right hand man and administered a famine relief program. The book of Genesis closes with the entire family joining Joseph in Egypt to escape the famine in Canaan. Genesis 46:27 tells us that by the time Jacob and the other sons and their families joined Joseph there was a total of seventy of them in Egypt.

Most dispensationalists consider this move to Egypt by the entire group of Abraham's descendants to be the failure for this dispensation. They disobeyed the command to dwell in Canaan. Some, however, have wondered whether this should be considered a failure of the test because before leaving for Egypt God told Jacob, "Do not be afraid to go down to Egypt, for I will make you into a great nation there. I will go down to Egypt with you, and I will surely bring you back again. And Joseph's own hand will close your eyes" (Gen. 46:3,4). This objection has weight, but it is significant that in Galatians 3:15-19 Paul seems to draw a natural line between the period of the promise given to Abraham and the period of the law given to Moses. Ezekiel 20:8-10 describes the time spent in Egypt as a judgment during which God's wrath was poured out on His people because of disobedience.

Scripture has many examples where God graciously takes disobedient behavior which must be judged and at the same time works it out for overall benefit. Moses struck the rock in Numbers 20 instead of speaking to it as instructed. He was denied the right to enter the land as a result, but God still provided water for the people. Naomi and her husband, Elimelech, moved to Moab in the period of the judges, and while the judgment of God came on their household, it also resulted in Ruth becoming a part of the family tree of Christ.

A third reason for understanding the move to Egypt as the failure for this fourth dispensation is the result which followed. The family of seventy grew into a great nation during the 400 years they spent there, but they suffered under cruel slavery. This oppression by the Egyptians serves, then, as the judgment for what is known as the dispensation of Promise. It has been named this because of the great promises God made to Abraham when He called him in Genesis 12. Another noteworthy feature of this dispensation is the new nature of Party #2. Up until this time God had dealt with all humankind, but here in His sovereignty He restricts His dealings to Abraham and his descendants. When charted as before we get the following:

Name	Innocence	Conscience	Human Gov't	Promise
Test	Fill, Subdue, Don't Eat	Obey Conscience	Fill and Subdue	Dwell in Canaan
Failure	Ate	EVIL!	Gathering at Babel	Moved to Egypt
Judgment	Cast out, Pain & Toil, Death	Flood	Confusion of Languages	400 Years of Slavery
Party #2	Adam & Eve	Humankind	Humankind	Abraham and Descendants

Figure 3.e

The fifth dispensation, Law, formally began at Sinai in Exodus 19. God led the people of Israel out of Egypt and brought them to Mount Sinai to receive the set of over 600 commandments which was to govern their lives both individually and nationally. Is perfect obedience to all of these laws the test for this *oikonomia*? No, because no one is capable of complete conformity to all the Law. The portion of the Law known as the Ten Commandments sets an absolute standard of righteousness which Paul says none can achieve (see Rom. 3:20). In fact, a primary ingredient in the Law was a system of sacrifices to make atonement for the inability to keep all of its commands.

The test for the dispensation of Law is specifically given in Exodus 19:5,6: "Now if you obey me fully and keep my covenant, then out of all nations you will be my treasured possession. Although the whole earth is mine, you will be for me a kingdom of priests and a holy nation." Certainly, the Mosaic Law formed a part of the test, and Israel was expected to offer the sacrifices to cover their failure to obey the commandments. But the test is larger than that. God told the nation Israel, the new Party #2, that they would be His special people if they obeyed Him fully, in every command or instruction given them. If at any time God asks Israel to do something, anything, they should respond with complete obedience. In return for this total obedience Israel will stand in a uniquely blessed relationship with God.

Because Israel is Party #2 in this fifth dispensation, the rest of the Old Testament focuses on their relationship with God. Deuteronomy 7:6 says, "For you are a people holy to the LORD your God. The LORD your God has chosen you out of all the peoples on the face of the earth to be his people, his treasured possession." In Romans 9:4,5, Paul gives a summary of the benefits Israel received because of her unique position. "Theirs is the adoption as sons; theirs the divine glory, the covenants, the receiving of the law, the temple worship and the promises. Theirs are the patriarchs, and from them is traced the human ancestry of Christ, who is God over all, forever praised! Amen." In sovereign grace God chose Israel as the recipients of His blessings and gave them a position above all other nations. Anyone outside of Israel, a Gentile, could only come to God through them.

Despite these blessings we see a pattern of failure, beginning with the golden calf which was set up by the people before Moses was even down from the Mount. However, God in His grace did not sever the relationship but continued to deal with them as His special people.

This relationship has clearly changed! In Paul's letters to the churches we read that the Jew no longer has advantage over the Gentile; both come to God equally. Galatians 3:28 says, "There is neither Jew nor Greek, slave nor free, male nor female, for you are all one in Christ Jesus." In Colossians 3:11 we read, "Here there is no Greek or Jew, circumcised or uncircumcised, barbarian, Scythian, slave or free, but Christ is all, and is in all." These passages and many others like them in Paul's letters present a clear contrast to the status Israel held in the Old Testament.

It could certainly not have been said there was no difference between Jew and Gentile during the time Israel was entering the Promised Land, for example. The reason for this dramatic change is that God has severed His dispensational relationship with Israel and begun a new *oikonomia* in which Party #2 is again all of humankind. When we read in Romans 10:12, "For there is no difference between Jew and Gentile—the same Lord is Lord of all and richly blesses all who call on him," it is obvious a dispensational change has been made.

When did this change occur, and what did Israel do to bring it about? A number of different views have been proposed and we will discuss them in some detail in our next chapter. For now we will leave that box on our chart open. But we can see that at least by the time Paul wrote his letters we have moved into a new dispensation in which Party #2 is all of humankind without regard for national origin (see Figure 3.f).

What is the test, or specific responsibility, for this current *oikonomia*? A survey of the epistles seems to indicate the test is simply to accept by faith Jesus Christ as personal Savior. God asks nothing more of humankind than that they "believe on the Lord Jesus Christ and be saved" (Acts 16:31). Those who do so become members of the Church, the Body of Christ. Note that Party #2 is not the Body of Christ, it is all humanity. The Body of Christ is only that portion of humanity who respond in faith to the offer of salvation through Christ.

Despite all of the millions over the centuries who have accepted God's gift of salvation, it is apparent the vast majority of humanity continues in sinful

Name	Innocence	Conscience	Human Gov't	Promise	Law
Test	Fill, Subdue, Don't Eat	Obey Conscience	Fill and Subdue	Dwell in Canaan	Obey God Fully
Failure	Ate	EVIL!	Gathering at Babel	Moved to Egypt	
Judgment	Cast out, Pain & Toil, Death	Flood	Confusion of Languages	400 Years of Slavery	Set Aside
Party #2	Adam & Eve	Humankind	Humankind	Abraham and Descendants	Israel

Figure 3.f

rebellion. As with all previous dispensations, this one also ends in failure. Again, we will discuss this in more detail in a future chapter, but this current dispensation will conclude with the removal of all believers to heaven through what is called the Rapture. The Tribulation will follow, a time described in Scripture as one during which God pours out His wrath on humankind (Rev. 6:16,17).

The seven-year Tribulation is the subject of several Old Testament prophetic passages which warn Israel about the time of trouble which will come to her (see Jer. 30:4-7 and Joel 2 as examples). It serves as a purifying fire to purge Israel and prepare her to once again receive God's special blessings. However, both Matthew 24 and the book of Revelation describe the Tribulation as bringing judgment on the whole earth through wars, natural disasters, and the outpouring of Satan's wickedness. Thus there is reason to think it also serves a second purpose—the judgment for this dispensation. If this is the case we must assume the Tribulation will begin shortly after the Rapture. As the ark delivered Noah and his family from the judgment of the flood, so the Rapture delivers believers from the judgment of the Tribulation.

Others view the Tribulation as something wholly Jewish in its significance. It is called the "time of trouble for Jacob" (Jer. 30:7), and Israel is the special focus of Satan's attack. According to this view the Tribulation will begin at least a full generation after the Rapture, and the judgment for this dispensation is that the unsaved will be left without a witness during that time. For the sake of simplicity our chart will reflect the former view.

This dispensation in which we are currently living is known as the dispensation of Grace, from Paul's expression in Ephesians 3:2, "Surely you have heard about the administration [*oikonomia*] of God's grace that was given to me for you." This name does not mean that salvation by God's grace is something peculiar to this dispensation. The term "grace" focuses on the special blessing of God which opens the way for the Gentile to come to him on an equal basis with the Jew.

After the Tribulation comes the return of Christ to set up the seventh and final *oikonomia*, known as the dispensation of the Kingdom. The Old Testament prophets predicted, and Revelation 20 describes, His coming to earth to reign in Jerusalem over all the earth. Israel will once again be God's special people and enjoy all the privileges promised by the prophets (see Zech. 8:20-23). The test, however, will be given to all humankind and consists of submitting to the reign and authority of Christ. In Psalm 2:12, David speaks prophetically of this time when he urges the nations to "Kiss the Son, lest he be angry and you be destroyed in your way." But, as Revelation 20 tells us, Satan, who has been bound for 1,000 years, is released and immediately leads the world in rebellion against Christ. This failure is immediately followed by the judgment known as the battle of Gog and Magog (Rev. 20:7-9). See Figure 3.g.

This brings human history to an end. After a series of seven dispensations, God brings all things to conclusion and administers the final judgment at the Great White Throne (Rev. 20:11-15). He then creates the new heavens and the new earth, and

Name	Innocence	Conscience	Human Gov't	Promise	Law	Grace	Millennial Kingdom
Test	Fill, Subdue, Don't Eat	Obey Conscience	Fill and Subdue	Dwell in Canaan	Obey God Fully	Accept Salvation	Submit to His Reign
Failure	Ate	EVIL!	Gathering at Babel	Moved to Egypt		Reject Salvation	Rebel under Satan
Judgment	Cast out, Pain & Toil, Death	Flood	Confusion of Languages	400 Years of Slavery	Set Aside	Tribulation	Destroyed in Battle
Party #2	Adam & Eve	Humankind	Humankind	Abraham and Descendants	Israel	Humankind	Humankind

Figure 3.g

what we call eternity begins. But the repeated pattern of test, failure, judgment is apparent as God has dealt with humankind through the dynamic of the *oikonomia*.

This overview of the dispensations shows how essential it is to distinguish between vertical and horizontal truths in order to conform to God's will for us. Because certain commands were intended only for the dispensation in which they were given, we would be in error if we tried to bring them into this dispensation. Consider the foolishness of trying to obey God's order to go to Canaan and dwell there. But we would also miss the mark if we did not carry out instructions which God meant as horizontal and therefore applicable in all dispensations.

This means it is important to clearly and accurately understand precisely when the change from the dispensation of Law to the dispensation of Grace took place. Vertical commands given at a point in time, during Christ's earthly ministry, for example, would be binding on us if this current dispensation had already begun. However, if the dispensation of Grace did not begin until after the earthly ministry of Christ, then at least some of what He instructed may be vertical, intended only for the previous dispensation and not applicable to us.

Because this is such an important issue and has led to considerable disagreement among Christians, we will take the next chapter to look carefully at when the dispensational change between Law and Grace took place. But before we do, here are the seven dispensations presented in chronological order in a time line format. This should prove helpful

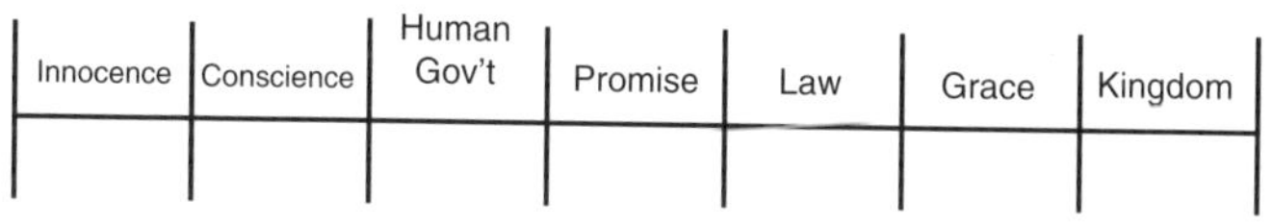

Innocence	Conscience	Human Gov't	Promise	Law	Grace	Kingdom

Figure 3.h

in nailing down the starting point of this present dispensation.

STUDY QUESTIONS

1. What is Charles Ryrie's helpful definition of a dispensation?
2. What do we mean by the term *vertical instruction*?
3. Name the seven dispensations in chronological order.
4. Who was Party #2 in the fifth dispensation?
5. How has that changed?

- Chapter 4 -

NAILING DOWN THE START

Locating the beginning point for this dispensation

When I was a child I had a red letter edition of the Bible. I knew the words in the Gospels printed with red ink were the words Christ spoke, and that filled me with awe. I unconsciously gave to them a higher level of importance and authority than the words in black. As I matured in the faith I came to understand that all Scripture is God-breathed and therefore every bit as authoritative as any other portion. The words Christ spoke were no more or less the words of God than those of Zechariah, Peter, or Paul when they wrote under the inspiration of the Holy Spirit. For this reason I now question the wisdom of red letter Bibles. How many children (or adults) are assuming the same thing I did, and as a result unconsciously devaluing the rest of God's Word? I suspect there is within many believers the sense that because we call ourselves Christians we have a special obligation to know and submit to the teachings of Christ given during His earthly ministry, even above those found elsewhere in Scripture.

HORIZONTAL OR VERTICAL?

Thus far we have learned God is dealing with humankind through a series of dispensations, each with its own unique set of responsibilities. As a result, the careful Bible student must not only ask "What is written?" but "To whom is it written?" If it was written to people living under a previous dispensation we must carefully determine whether or not the instructions are horizontal and apply to God's people of all ages, or vertical and intended only for those under that particular *oikonomia*.

The easiest way to determine if a particular instruction is vertical is to see if it is countermanded or changed in any way in a later dispensation. For example, in Genesis 9:3 God tells Noah, "Everything that lives and moves will be food for you. Just as I gave you the green plants, I now give you everything." However, in Deuteronomy 14 we read a long list of foods which may and may not be eaten by the people of Israel, a list which begins, "Do not eat any detestable thing" (Deut. 14:3). Then the apostle Paul tells Timothy, "Everything God created is good, and nothing is to be rejected if it is received with thanksgiving, because it is consecrated by the word of God and prayer" (1 Tim. 4:4,5). Here is a clear case of food instructions changing with the dispensations. Usually, as with this example, it is fairly clear which instructions are horizontal, applying to all dispensations, and which have been changed and are therefore vertical.

Back to my red letter Bible. Are the teachings of Christ authoritative for Christians today? (Are they horizontal?) In order to answer that question we need to determine the dispensation to which Christ came. What *oikonomia* was in effect when the Son of God entered time and space? Was it the same dispensation as the current one? And if not, did Christ act and teach within the guidelines of the previous dispensation or was everything He said and did horizontal in nature? The same question should be asked about the teachings of the apostles in the book of Acts and in the Epistles. It comes down to the question, "When did the change from the previous dispensation, Law, to the current dispensation, Grace, take place?" Our answer to that question will govern the way we understand God's will for ourselves and other believers.

Wherever the change takes place, all instructions given from that point until the end of this dispensation, whether vertical or horizontal, are binding upon believers in this dispensation. Instructions prior to that point may or may not apply to us depending on whether they are horizontal or vertical. A diagram which portrays this important question in the form of a time line may be helpful.

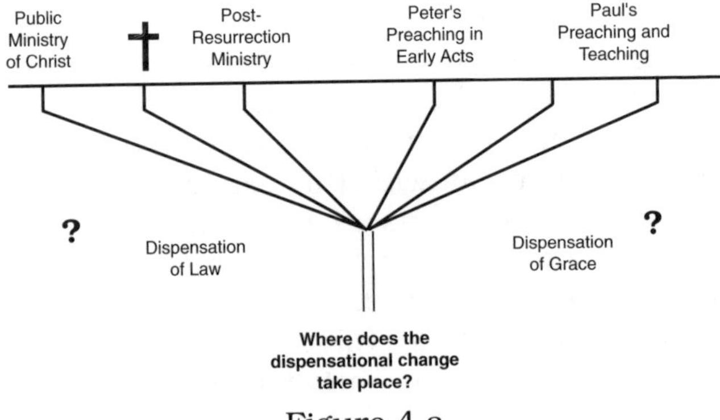

Figure 4.a

At which of the points shown did the change from the dispensation of Law to the dispensation of Grace take place? Because this period of biblical history is so loaded with instructional material the answer to this question is more than academic! Remember, commands given to the left of the dividing line may well be vertical and intended only for the dispensation of Law.

LOCATING THE POINT OF CHANGE

One of the methods which will *not* work for locating the point of dispensational change is looking for the word "church." Many people assume because they attend a church, and because Christ and Paul both talk about the church, the word "church" can serve to identify the point in time when God stopped dealing with the nation Israel and began dealing with all humankind without distinction. Thus, some think when we read in the Bible about the church we have come to this current dispensation.

Unfortunately, it is not that simple. In our current vocabulary the English word "church" has a religious meaning. We don't call union halls churches and we don't even use the word "church" to describe where the Jewish people meet; we call that a synagogue. For us, the word church refers exclusively to a Christian congregation and the building in which they meet. But the word "church" in our English Bibles is the Greek word *ekklesia*, and it is a much more generic term. Its literal meaning is "called out group" and it was used in the first century to describe any group of people who came together for any specific purpose. For example, in Acts 19:32 Luke uses *ekklesia* to describe the rioting mob in Ephesus: "The assembly [*ekklesia*] was in confusion: some were shouting one thing, some another." In verses 39 and 41 the mob is called an *ekklesia* by both Luke and the city clerk who addresses them. The NIV uses the word "assembly" in these verses as does the KJV because to call the mob a church would confuse us. But the Greek word is identical. Stephen in his speech in Acts 7 uses the word *ekklesia* to refer to Israel in the Old Testament. In verse 38 Stephen says, "He [Moses] was in the congregation [*ekklesia*] in the desert." Here Israel is referred to as a "church." The same thing occurs in Hebrews 2:12 where a quotation from Psalm 22:22 uses *ekklesia* to refer to Israel.

Because the word *ekklesia* can mean anything from a rioting mob to the assembled nation of Israel we should not use it to identify the point of dispensational change. So, for example, when Christ says, "you are Peter, and on this rock I will build my church" (Matt.16:18) we should not automatically assume He is referring to the same body of believers of this current dispensation known as the Body of Christ. The same care must be used when reading Acts 5:11, "Great fear seized the whole church and all who heard about these events." This may or may not be the Body of Christ. It could just as easily refer to a particular group of Jews under the dispensation of Law. The matter of when God set Israel aside and began the dispensation of Grace is one which the Bible answers, but using the generic term *ekklesia* isn't the key.

A word which *is* important in this discussion is the Greek word *musterion*, which serves as the source for our English word "mystery." In contrast to the generic term *ekklesia*, *musterion* has a very narrow meaning. One of its applications in New Testament times was in connection with what we now call "mystery religions." These were first century cults in which the members took very strict vows of secrecy, promising never to reveal the rites and membership of their group. This usage illustrates that the word *musterion* has the same meaning as our word "secret," namely something which is totally unknown to those outside the informed person or group. Of course, if God has a *musterion*, or secret, He is the informed Person and it is unknown to all humankind until the time He chooses to reveal it. Special revelation will be required for humankind to know God's secret, because no amount of effort on humankind's part could ever discover a *musterion* of God.

The significance of all this is that the apostle Paul uses the word *musterion* to describe the current dispensation in which God no longer deals with Israel as His special people but instead treats all humankind equally. In Ephesians 3:6 Paul says, "This mystery [*musterion*] is that through the gospel the Gentiles are heirs together with Israel, members together of one body, and sharers together in the promise in Christ Jesus." It was a secret known only to God that He would one day suspend His relationship with Israel as a privileged people and open His dealings to all humankind like He did before Abraham.

Nowhere in the prophetic passages of the Old Testament is there any indication God would set Israel aside as His people and again deal for a time with Jew and Gentile equally. Certainly the Old Testament *does* record and predict Gentile salvation, but when it happens it is through Israel, who acts as God's evangelizing agent (see Zech. 8:23 as an example).

The Old Testament presents an outline of human history which centers around an unbroken relationship between God and the nation Israel as His unique people. Note the contrast between passages like Deuteronomy 7:6, "The LORD your God has chosen you out of all the peoples on the face of the earth to be his people, his treasured possession," and Colossians 3:11, "Here there is no Greek or Jew, circumcised or uncircumcised, barbarian, Scythian, slave or free, but Christ is all, and is in all." The Jew/Gentile equality which is the distinguishing feature of this present dispensation was a secret, a *musterion* known only to God until He chose to reveal it. In Colossians 1:26-27 Paul says, ". . . the mystery that has been kept hidden for ages and generations, but is now disclosed to the saints. To them God has chosen to make known among the Gentiles the glorious riches of this mystery, which is Christ in you the hope of glory." Thus, this present dispensation where Jew and Gentile are equal, and the called out group (*ekklesia*) within it, known as the Body of Christ, were a mystery until their revelation from God.

Identifying the point in time when this revelation was given will serve as a key tool in locating the beginning of the dispensation of Grace. It is reasonable to assume God would reveal the secret of Jew/Gentile equality (that is, the temporary setting aside of Israel as His special people) at the same point in time He ends the dispensation of Law and begins the dispensation of Grace. Fortunately, Scripture is very clear in telling us who received the revelation of the mystery—who was given the instructions for this dispensation. It was none other than the apostle Paul.

In fact, Paul goes to great lengths to make it clear he was the one to receive this *musterion* from God. In Ephesians 3:2,3 he writes, "Surely you have heard about the administration of God's grace *that was given to me for you*, that is, the mystery made known to me by revelation, as I have already written briefly." He told the Galatians, "I want you to know, brothers, that the gospel I preached is not something that man made up. I did not receive it from any man, nor was I taught it; rather I received it by revelation from Jesus Christ" (Gal. 1:11,12). And so it was not arrogance but rather Paul's awareness of his unique role in God's plan which led him to use the term "my gospel" in Romans 16:25, "Now to him who is able to establish you by *my* gospel and the proclamation of Jesus Christ, according to the revelation of the mystery hidden for long ages past . . . ." In the Colossians passage referred to earlier Paul writes, "I have become its [the church's] servant by the commission God gave me to present to you the word of God in its fullness—the mystery that has been kept hidden for ages and generations, but is now disclosed to the saints" (Col. 1:25,26).

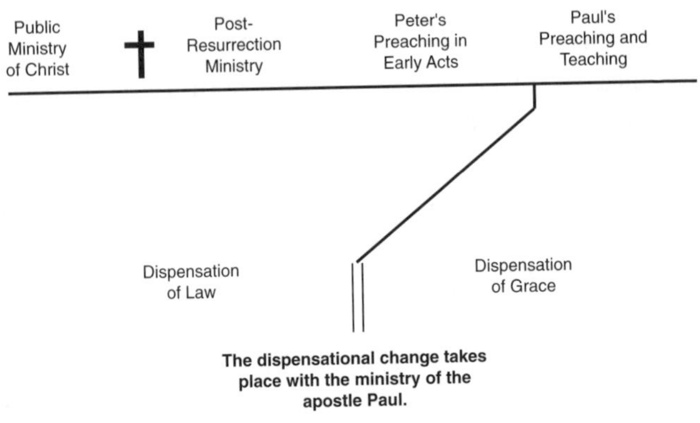

Figure 4.b

Paul's conversion on the road to Damascus (Acts 9) seems to have taken place within the context of the dispensation of Law. Aside from the remarkable circumstances, nothing about the experience looks any different from what had been taking place prior to this point in Acts. It looks like a conversion under the conditions of the dispensation of Law. But God does hint that He has a special role in mind for the apostle Paul. The Lord told Ananias, "Go! This man is my chosen instrument to carry my name before the Gentiles and their kings and before the people of Israel" (Acts 9:15). Note the order in which Gentiles and Jews are mentioned, and the striking contrast it is to conditions under the dispensation of Law.

When Paul recounts his conversion before the crowd in Acts 22 he records some of the words Christ spoke to him on the road: "'Get up,' the Lord said, 'and go into Damascus. There you will be told all that you have been assigned to do'" (v. 10). And at his trial before Agrippa we learn that Christ said to him, "Now get up and stand on your feet. I have appeared to you to appoint you as a servant and as a witness of what you have seen of me and what I will show you" (Acts 26:16).

Paul does not tell us specifically when he received the revelation of the mystery of this dispensation. One likely possibility is the three-year period of time he spent in Arabia right after his visit to Ananias in Damascus (see Gal. 1:17,18). But it is clear the revelation had been given to Paul by the time he left on his first missionary journey. The record of his ministry on that journey, including the sermon recorded in Acts 13, shows a clear change in God's dealings with humankind, specifically with the Gentiles.

OBSERVING THE CONTRASTS

Paul describes himself as the "apostle to the Gentiles" in Romans 11:13 and Galatians 2:8 because of his unique commission to tell the Gentiles about the gospel, the good news of salvation, and of God's grace toward them as He accepts them on a par with Israel. This equality was the mystery revealed to Paul. Thus, this present *oikonomia*, the dispensation of Grace, begins with the ministry of the apostle Paul sometime between his conversion in Acts 9 and his first missionary journey in Acts 13. We might well look to his time in Arabia as the specific point when the revelation of the mystery was given to him.

One obvious result of placing the beginning of this present dispensation at the time of the revelation of the mystery to Paul is the conclusion that all which immediately preceded him belongs to the previous dispensation, Law. That includes both the earthly ministry of Christ and the early chapters of the book of Acts. This conclusion is supported when we look at the material in these sections of the Bible. The content of biblical passages before Paul's ministry is clearly consistent with the terms and conditions of the dispensation of Law. In fact, much of the teaching in the Gospels and early Acts contrasts in important ways with the dispensation of Grace as outlined by Paul. But remember, there will always be horizontal truths.

One of the contrasts involves the matter of prophecy. Because prophecy and mystery are mutually exclusive (if it is prophesied it can't be a secret and vice versa), anything which involves the fulfillment of prophecies made to Israel or makes further promises to the nation is clearly within the boundaries of the dispensation of Law. The dispensation of Grace and its features were a mystery, "kept hidden in God, who created all things" (Eph. 3:9). Even a casual reading of the Gospels and the early chapters of Acts shows Israel's prophetic agenda was the basis for both the teachings and events of that period. Eleven times in Matthew's gospel he tells us a particular event happened in accordance with the prediction of a prophet (see Matt. 2:5,17 as examples). Christ warned the disciples to be on the lookout for the abomination of desolation spoken of by the prophet Daniel (Matt. 24:15).

This focus on prophecies to Israel can also be seen in early Acts. In Peter's first sermon (chapter 2) he tells the crowd the events they are witnessing are the fulfillment of the prophecy given by the prophet Joel (see v. 16) whom he goes on to quote. Clearly God is here dealing with Israel under His special relationship with them just as He was in the Old Testament. In fact, He is beginning to fulfill promises made to Israel regarding the "last days" (v. 17). Peter's sermon climaxes with the proclamation that Jesus whom they crucified was the Christ or Messiah (v. 36), the One promised to Israel. Peter's sermon in chapter 3 is even more clearly a continuation of God's dealings with Israel. Peter again tells his listeners the crucifixion of Jesus was the fulfillment of prophecies made to their forefathers (vv. 17,18). In verses 24 and 25 He says, "Indeed, all the prophets from Samuel on, as many as have spoken, have foretold these days. And you are heirs of the prophets and of the covenant God made with your fathers. He said to Abraham, 'Through your offspring all peoples on earth will be blessed.'"

This emphasis on prophecy stands in clear contrast to Paul's emphasis that this dispensation was a mystery never before revealed through prophecy. The features and events of the dispensation of Grace cannot be found predicted on the pages of the Old Testament, nor unfolding during Christ's earthly ministry or during Peter's ministry in Acts. They were revealed first to the apostle Paul.

The only thing which changes between Malachi, the last book of the Old Testament, and Matthew, the first book in the New Testament, is the date. God was continuing to deal with Israel and doing so within the context of the prophecies and promises made to her. That is why it is not surprising to see in the Gospels and early chapters of Acts that

Israel continues to enjoy privileged status before God, holding a position as "his treasured possession" (Deut. 7:6).

Christ's earthly ministry was directed to the Jews and any contact He had with Gentiles is presented as a striking exception to His normal practice. In Matthew 23:2,3 Christ instructs His followers to obey the Pharisees, "and do everything they tell you." These Pharisees were the ones who taught the Jews to obey the Mosaic Law, including all the rituals, ceremonies, and holy days. Contrast this with Paul's instruction that we should not allow anyone to hold us accountable to the commands of the Law (Col. 2:16ff). Peter's ministry in Acts is also completely Jewish in both scope and content. His audience in Acts 2 was "men of Israel" (v. 22) and the occasion which brought them together was Pentecost, an annual Jewish feast. In chapter 3 Peter speaks to a crowd of Jews gathered at the temple and tells them to repent so they can receive the "times of refreshing" in order that God "may send the Christ [Messiah] who has been appointed for you" (vv. 19,20).

In Acts 5:12 we learn the believers were meeting at Solomon's Colonnade, an area within the temple grounds, and the problem in chapter 6 involved a disagreement between Jews, some of whom spoke Aramaic while others spoke Greek. The seven men chosen to help solve the problem were all Jews, including Nicolas, a convert to Judaism. It is very possible the Ethiopian eunuch in chapter 8 was a Jew who lived in Ethiopia. If not, he was certainly a proselyte or convert to Judaism, because he had gone to Jerusalem to worship.

In short, everything in the Gospels and the first eight chapters of Acts is consistent with God's continued dealings with the nation of Israel as His special people. God's prophetic agenda was continuing to unfold and the offer of the Messianic kingdom was being made to the Jews in the name of Jesus their Messiah.

This uninterrupted thread of ministry to and for Israel is abruptly broken with the chain of events which begins with Paul's conversion in chapter 9. Paul's account in Galatians chapter 1 traces his movements in those early months after his salvation. We learn that immediately following his short stay in Damascus he went out to the Arabian desert where he stayed for the better part of three years. "Then after three years, I went up to Jerusalem to get acquainted with Peter and stayed with him fifteen days" (v. 18). If Paul, during this stay in Arabia, had received the revelation of the mystery that God was beginning a new dispensation in which Jew and Gentile were equal before God, he would surely tell a shocked (and undoubtedly disbelieving) Peter during this fifteen-day visit. In Acts the account of Paul's conversion in chapter 9 is followed by Peter's visit to the Gentile Cornelius in chapter 10. But between these events is Paul's fifteen-day stay with Peter. When God tells Peter to go to Cornelius the Gentile, Peter is at first very reluctant to go, even though he had heard about the new dispensation from Paul. After some divine persuasion through the vision of the sheet, he goes, and when Cornelius and his household are saved Peter says, "I now realize how true it is that God does not show favoritism but accepts men from every nation who fear him and do what is right" (v. 34).

Those words represent a major change in Peter's theology from what he had been preaching to and for Israel in earlier chapters. Paul's news of a dispensational change had been confirmed to him by divine direction and he accepted it as from God. At this point the narrative of Acts shifts from a wholly Jewish perspective to one in which Jew and Gentile are saved without distinction.

Correctly placing the beginning of the dispensation of Grace with the ministry of the apostle Paul allows us to be more precise in distinguishing truths which do and do not apply to us today. It means we must read the Gospels and the first portion of Acts carefully so as not to apply vertical truths meant for Israel to the Body of Christ. Certainly our goal is to correctly handle the word of truth (2 Tim. 2:15), and this kind of dispensational accuracy is an important part of the effort. In a future chapter we will look at some of the specific consequences of a proper dispensational framework, one which recognizes Paul's role as God's instrument in beginning the dispensation of Grace.

STUDY QUESTIONS

1. What is the best way to identify vertical truths?
2. What is the meaning of *ekklesia* and how is it usually translated in the Bible?
3. Why does this word *not* work as a means of identifying the beginning of this dispensation?

4. What does the word *musterion* mean?
5. Why is this word the key to identifying the beginning of this dispensation?
6. When did the dispensation of Grace begin?
7. Name one of the implications of this fact.

- *Chapter 5* -

WHAT MUST I DO TO BE SAVED?

Salvation in Dispensationalism

In chapter one we mentioned the two basic hermeneutical options used when interpreting the Bible, the allegorical and the literal (normal) methods. In reality the two options are the two ends of a continuum, with everyone using the literal method to a greater or lesser degree.

Virtually all evangelical Bible students understand the historical sections of the Old Testament literally. Those biblical people, places, and events were real. It is primarily in the prophetic passages where a decision between the two options must be made.

Covenant theology is a type of theology which sees Scripture and human history as a single block with only one people of God, called Israel in the Old Testament and the Body of Christ in the New Testament. According to covenant theology the specific regulations of the Mosaic Law may no longer be in force, but the basic dynamics of God's relationship with humankind remain constant. In other words, what is said to Israel is said to the Body of Christ, including promises about future events. If that strikcs the reader as a problem, the covenant theologian would agree because the reader is interpreting things literally which God meant to be taken figuratively. For covenant theology the Bible's emphasis is on the spiritual dimension, not the physical. Therefore, prophecies which predict Christ's return to earth to establish a worldwide kingdom centered in Jerusalem should be interpreted figuratively and are meant to teach us about Christ's reign in the believer's life. Covenant theology is toward the allegorical end of the hermeneutics continuum.

As we have seen, dispensational theology uses a consistently literal or normal hermeneutic and as a result distinguishes between Israel and the Body of Christ. Promises made to Israel will be literally fulfilled one day, while the Body of Christ has a different agenda. We will examine the matter of future events in a later chapter, but what is apparent even at this point is that whereas covenant theology believes in *uniformity*, dispensational theology believes in *unity*. In other words, dispensational theology recognizes both the important constants which run throughout God's dealings with humankind, as well as the distinctions which exist as God deals differently in different *oikonomias*.

One of the criticisms covenant theologians have brought against dispensationalism is that the latter teaches multiple methods of salvation. The charge is that the dispensationalist believes the requirements for salvation have varied from dispensation to dispensation. Worse yet, the dispensationalist is accused of believing that during the dispensation of Law people were saved by obedience to the Law, that is, by works. Because such a notion is clearly contrary to the teachings of Scripture (see Gal. 3:11, for example), any system which would hold to such a view, it is said, is obviously in serious error.

These criticisms have been brought against dispensationalism for a couple of reasons. The first is that, sadly, some dispensationalists have taught the substitutionary death of Christ was part of the mystery revealed to the apostle Paul. They have implied, and in some cases actually said, that salvation prior to this dispensation did involve obedience to the Law. With this teaching we must strongly disagree! The apostle Paul would want no part of it, nor do we.

Another reason some have wrongly concluded dispensationalism teaches different ways of salvation is the name given to the current dispensation. We saw that the title "dispensation of Grace" comes from Paul's expression in Ephesians 3:2, "Surely you have heard about the administration [*oikonomia*] of God's grace that was given to me for you." So it is at least understandable when some get the impression dispensationalists believe there was no grace in previous dispensations, or that salvation before Paul was not by grace but by works.

As we have seen, Paul taught the Law's complete inability to bring about righteousness. In Romans 3:20 he writes, "Therefore no one will be declared righteous in his sight by observing the law; rather through the law we become conscious of sin."

Then why does Paul himself call this the dispensation of Grace? It is not because God's grace appears for the first time, but because it appears to such a great extent.

The 1980s were called by many the "me" decade. It was certainly not the first time humankind's inborn selfishness appeared, but it was a period in which it seemed to be especially evident. This is similar to the matter of God's grace throughout history. In every era of human history we read of God's grace toward humankind. He allows us life, He sends rain and sunshine in appropriate measure, He ordains governments for our protection, and much, much more. But in this dispensation God shows equal favor to Jew and Gentile alike without distinction. To those of us outside of Israel and the privileges which were hers alone, this is a tremendous manifestation of God's grace. We remember, as Paul says in Ephesians 2:12,13, that we as Gentiles, "were separate from Christ, excluded from citizenship in Israel and foreigners to the covenants of the promise, without hope and without God in the world. But now in Christ Jesus you who once were far away have been brought near through the blood of Christ." Thus it is appropriate for Paul to call this the *oikonomia* of God's grace because grace is so apparent in this dispensation as God reaches out to Gentiles. And when we follow Paul's lead we in no way imply there was no grace prior to this dispensation, nor that salvation was gained through any other means. Careful dispensationalists believe all the redeemed in every dispensation are saved by God's grace and not in any sense through their own works.

Does that mean dispensationalism and covenant theology are in agreement about how humankind has received salvation throughout history? No, it does not, because there is another question having to do with salvation besides the matter of grace versus works. It relates to the concept known as progressive revelation.

We have learned that each dispensation contains its own set of responsibilities. The set for a new dispensation may continue some responsibilities from the previous dispensation, delete others, and add still others. This change is accomplished through revelation as God supernaturally communicates His will for that particular *oikonomia* to its Party #2 or a representative who then communicates it to others. For example, God spoke to Noah after the flood to give him the terms and conditions for the dispensation of Human Government (Gen. 9:1-7). He called Moses up to Mt. Sinai and revealed to him the responsibilities which were Israel's as God's Party #2 in the dispensation of Law, and He revealed to Paul the truths for the dispensation of Grace which Paul then preached everywhere he traveled.

As each succeeding revelation was given, humankind gained a more complete understanding of God and His ways. And as God revealed the terms and conditions for the dispensations He also opened up to humankind the means by which He would provide full atonement for sin. After Adam and Eve's sin God told Satan, "I will put enmity between you and the woman, and between your offspring and hers; he will crush your head, and you will strike his heel" (Gen. 3:15). Bible scholars call this verse the *protoevangelium*, the first mention of the gospel. While we notice the woman's seed, or offspring, will crush not the serpent's seed, but the serpent himself, this verse leaves many questions unanswered, such as the identity of the woman's seed. It is only a hint of a victory over Satan which will come some day and in a way which was left unexplained to Adam and Eve.

As time went on, more and more of God's plan for salvation was presented. That is, it was given through progressive revelation. Abraham was told all peoples on earth would be blessed through him, indicating the Savior would come through his lineage. Moses said, "The scepter will not depart from Judah, nor the ruler's staff from between his feet, until he comes to whom it belongs" (Gen. 49:10), thus revealing the Redeemer would come from the tribe of Judah. In Isaiah 7:14 we learn God will come in the flesh through a virgin birth. In Micah 5:2 we learn the birth will take place in Bethlehem.

But it was not until Jesus Christ actually came to earth and died on the cross that the full picture of God's provision was clear. In fact, after His resurrection Christ found it necessary to explain to His disciples the Old Testament prophecies concerning His death and its significance.

> He said to them, "This is what I told you while I was still with you: Everything must be fulfilled that is written about me in the Law of Moses, the Prophets and the Psalms." Then he opened their minds so they could understand the Scriptures. He told them, "This is what is written: The Christ will suffer and rise from the dead on the third day, and repentance and forgiveness of sins will be

preached in his name to all nations, beginning at Jerusalem" (Luke 24:44-47).

Paul says the Old Testament ordinances were a "shadow of the things that were to come; the reality, however, is found in Christ" (Col. 2:17). Thus, the term "progressive revelation" in this context means the doctrine of salvation through faith in the death, burial, and resurrection of Christ was revealed in increments, progressively building an expanding picture which reached complete clarity only after His redemptive work was finished. Progressive revelation also continued with regard to other truths, including the revelation of the mystery given to the apostle Paul.

The position of covenant theology is quite different. It believes in uniformity—that God has always had just one people and has always dealt with them in the same way. All revealed truth has been known in all ages. Thus, the covenant theologian believes Adam knew and understood all about Christ's redemptive work just as we do. Whereas we know it by looking back, Adam and all other Old Testament saints knew it by looking ahead. Covenant theology maintains God had revealed to Adam and all his descendants the complete picture of both Christ's work and its significance.

The covenant theologian Charles Hodge in his *Systematic Theology* says, "There is not a doctrine concerning Christ, taught in the New Testament, which the Apostles do not affirm to have been revealed under former dispensations. They therefore distinctly assert that it was through Him and the efficacy of his death that men were saved before, as well as after his advent" (vol. 2, pages 370,371).

Thus, the covenant theologian, when asked the question, "How are individuals saved?" gives one answer for all of human history. He responds that all people in all ages have been saved by believing Christ died for their sins. Why, then, is not the full plan of redemption clear to us as we read the Old Testament? The covenant theologian would answer by saying God chose to explain it to the readers of the Old Testament (us) gradually, despite the fact the Old Testament saints themselves understood it fully. Thus, the covenant position might be termed progressive explanation.

How does the dispensationalist answer the question "How are individuals saved?" In keeping with the principle of unity the answer is, "By God's grace through faith." But the object of that faith has changed. Since the time of the Cross the object of faith has been Christ and His redemptive work. Before the Cross people were unaware of His yet-to-come salvation work and therefore the object of their faith was necessarily different. What was it?

SALVATION BEFORE THE CROSS

Paul tells us "the wages of sin is death" (Rom. 6:23). In Hebrews 9:22 we read, "In fact, the law requires that nearly everything be cleansed with blood, and without the shedding of blood there is no forgiveness." These and many other passages teach us that where there is sin there must be punishment, and the divinely prescribed punishment for sin is death. It is significant that the first death recorded in Scripture is the death of the animals

God killed after Adam and Eve sinned in order to make coverings for them (Gen. 3:21). This event is important in light of the truth just mentioned: where there is sin there must be the penalty of death, the shedding of blood. The animals died so the effects (both physical and spiritual) of Adam and Eve's sin could be covered.

Immediately after the account in Genesis 3 is the record of Cain's murder of Abel. The cause of Cain's anger toward his brother was God's acceptance of Abel's blood sacrifice and the rejection of his own offering of crops. Why was one offering accepted and another rejected? Because even at this early point God had apparently revealed that blood sacrifices were to be brought. So from the very beginning God instructed, and obedient people offered up animals as payment for sins. The animals (which had to be "clean" as defined by God) served as substitutes, dying in the place of the offerer.

This unbroken chain of blood sacrifices continues through Noah, who offered up animals immediately after leaving the ark, and the patriarchs who sacrificed to the Lord. All of these generations uniformly brought blood sacrifices despite the fact no specific command for them to do so is recorded in Scripture. Their actions probably trace back to an instruction given to Adam which was passed down orally through the generations.

The religious commandments given to Israel at Sinai set out for the first time specific written instructions on the offerings to be brought, their type, frequency, and manner of offering. An example of these instructions is the section which begins in Leviticus 4. In each case the one bringing the sin offering is to bring the appropriate animal to the altar and lay his hands on the head of the animal. Why? This action symbolically transfers the guilt of the offerer to the animal about to be slain. The animal dies as his substitute. Prior to the Cross God accepted the sacrifice of clean animals as a temporary covering for the sins of the offerer.

However, this does not mean everyone who brought an animal sacrifice was saved. In Isaiah 1:11 we read, "'The multitude of your sacrifices—what are they to me?' says the LORD. 'I have more than enough of burnt offerings, of rams and the fat of fattened animals; I have no pleasure in the blood of bulls and lambs and goats.'" God did not accept Israel's offerings in Isaiah's day because as Isaiah goes on to explain, they were brought as meaningless religious ritual. The missing ingredient was faith. "And without faith it is impossible to please God" (Heb. 11:6).

How were Old Testament saints saved? The dispensationalist who sees progressive revelation as a key part of God's dealings with humankind answers the question in a way consistent with the principle of unity. Old Testament saints were saved as they brought the appropriate blood sacrifices, in faith believing God accepted the offering as the temporary payment for their sins. But as we read in Hebrews 10:4, "it is impossible for the blood of bulls and goats to take away sins." So, "when the time had fully come, God sent his Son, born of a woman, born under law, to redeem those under law, that we might receive the full rights of sons" (Gal. 4:4,5).

Works have never had any role in man's salvation. Redemption has always been by grace through faith in a sacrificial substitute. Prior to the Cross the substitute was the animal offered. But because animals are inadequate to pay for the sins of humankind, God sent His Son, Jesus Christ as the only adequate sacrifice. Thus, only the object of faith has changed, from animals to the Son of God.

SALVATION AND THE DISPENSATIONAL TEST

At this point it is helpful to note the relationship between the test in the various dispensations and the matter of salvation. Specifically, in all dispensations except this present one the dispensational test and salvation are completely separate issues, making it possible to fail the test and still be redeemed. In the first dispensation, Innocence, Adam and Eve failed the test, yet it is probable they are eternally saved by virtue of the blood which was shed on their behalf. Abraham's descendants left Canaan, the land allotted to them, and moved as a group to Egypt, apparently with the intention of settling there permanently. They thus failed to carry out the specific responsibilities given to them. However, we expect to see most of the group of seventy (see Gen. 46:26,27) in glory. And while Israel as a nation failed their responsibility to obey God fully (Ex. 19:5,6) there are certainly many individuals who were redeemed.

The key to this dynamic is in understanding that salvation is and always has been a matter of the *individual's* relationship with God. Every man and woman is by nature a sinner. As we have seen, the wages of sin is death and only the shedding of blood can atone for sin. Before the Cross the individual was saved by believing the animal offered was dying as a substitute, whereas since the Cross the individual's faith is in the perfect and adequate death of Jesus Christ.

Separate from this individual salvation is the dispensational relationship in which God deals with a *group* as Party #2 and the group fails or succeeds as a whole. The nation Israel failed to obey God fully, and therefore, despite the fact God never even hinted He might do so, He set them aside as His special people. Thus, an individual Jew in Old Testament or early New Testament times might be in right relationship with God in terms of his individual condition because of his saving faith, and yet still be part of a nation which was out of favor with God and being set aside as His privileged people.

Only in this dispensation of Grace is the test the same as the criterion for individual salvation. But even here God deals with all of humanity as Party #2 and determines obedience based on the response of the whole. While millions of people over the last 2,000 years have heard and received the good news of salvation through the substitutionary death of Christ, the vast majority of humankind during the same period comes under Paul's pronouncement in Romans 1:22,23, "Although they claimed to be wise, they became fools and exchanged the glory of the immortal God for images made to look like mortal man and birds and animals and reptiles." As a result of this rebellion God will, in His own sovereign time, bring judgment upon humankind.

WHY IT IS IMPORTANT

The reason for distinguishing between the dispensational test and the matter of individual salvation becomes clear when we realize that some things are secondary aspects of salvation and not related to the dispensations. The indwelling Holy Spirit within every believer is an example of this. God cannot dwell or reside in the individual whose sins have not been covered. To do so would violate His holiness. The sins of humankind were not paid for prior to Christ's death on the cross, because, as Hebrews 10:4 says, the blood of bulls and goats cannot take away sins. Even those who had faith in the animal sacrifice they offered were not fully righteous in His sight. God was graciously accepting their offering as a temporary and inadequate covering until the time of the permanent and perfect sacrifice of Christ.

Because the Old Testament saints were not righteous in His sight the Holy Spirit did not, could not, permanently indwell them as He does saints after the Cross. We read of the Spirit of the Lord coming upon them, as with Samson (Judges 14:6), but He also later left. David prayed, "Do not cast me from your presence or take your Holy Spirit from me" (Ps. 51:11). The Holy Spirit came upon Old Testament individuals at particular times in order to equip them for particular tasks. When the task was accomplished, or they had disqualified themselves through disobedience, the Spirit left them.

Since Christ's death, burial, and resurrection believers have complete forgiveness of all sins (Col. 2:13). We have been justified by His blood (Rom. 5:9) and are free from any condemnation (Rom. 8:1).

Thus, the Holy Spirit can and does permanently indwell every believer so that Paul can say, "If anyone does not have the Spirit of Christ, he does not belong to Christ" (Rom. 8:9).

God chose a specific point in time to pour out His Spirit on those who believe, and it was the feast of Pentecost as recorded in Acts 2. On that day, fifty days after Christ's crucifixion and ten days after His ascension, He fulfilled the promise given in John 16:7, "Unless I go away, the Counselor will not come to you; but if I go, I will send him to you." Peter reminds his listeners at Pentecost that the outpouring of the Holy Spirit was prophesied by Joel (an obvious contrast with a mystery never before revealed). But note that the giving of the Holy Spirit was related not to dispensational dynamics but to the matter of salvation, specifically salvation's completion through the work of Christ.

Many dispensationalists place the beginning of the current dispensation at Pentecost in Acts 2. They do this because the indwelling Holy Spirit is a key truth for this age, one which Paul frequently stresses. Paul says in 1 Corinthians 6:19, "Do you not know that your body is a temple of the Holy Spirit, who is in you, whom you have received from God?" But the Holy Spirit's indwelling is not the distinguishing feature of the dispensation of Grace. It is not a dispensationally related truth at all; it is instead connected with the doctrine of salvation. The distinguishing feature of this dispensation is Jew/Gentile equality, a mystery revealed first to the apostle Paul.

Pentecost was not the beginning point for the dispensation of Grace or the Body of Christ. It was the point in time fifty days after Christ's death at Passover when God gave to those *individuals* who accepted the gift of righteousness by faith the permanently indwelling Holy Spirit. Dispensationally God was still dealing with the nation of Israel, as we have seen. Was there any significance to the events of that day for the nation Israel? There certainly was, and that is our next topic.

STUDY QUESTIONS

1. Why does Paul call this the dispensation of Grace?
2. What does the term *progressive revelation* mean?
3. What do covenant theologians believe about how people were saved before the cross?
4. What do dispensational theologians believe about how people were saved before the Cross?
5. What is the relationship between the dispensational test and salvation? Explain your answer.
6. Why is the giving of the indwelling Holy Spirit in Acts 2 *not* a basis for beginning the dispensation of Grace and the Body of Christ at that point?

- Chapter 6 -

LOOKING TO THE FUTURE

Different dispensations, different futures

Some human beings are by nature very easy going and relaxed. These people take things as they come, are rarely flustered, and seem to have mastered the truth of Matthew 6:34, "Therefore do not worry about tomorrow, for tomorrow will worry about itself. Each day has enough trouble of its own."

Others of us come at life from a very different angle. We plan and organize down to the smallest detail well before any real need. If things don't go according to that plan it can send us into a tizzy, and woe be to the person responsible! There may be time to smell the roses later, but first they have to be weeded, pruned, and fertilized. It says so in my daily planner.

TWO VIEWS OF THE FUTURE

God has done many wonderful things for His people throughout history, each of them a proof of His grace. One blessing to believers of all personality types is telling us His plans for the future. Certainly all believers should trust God to complete the salvation which we have received in Christ, even if He gave no details about the when and how. He knows our weakness, and has provided us with an added measure of assurance by laying out in Scripture His blueprint for the future. Most of us would like even more detail than we have in the Bible, and what we read sometimes raises as many questions as it answers, but it is a blessing to have what God has chosen to reveal. We are confident that what He has said He will do, "for he who promised is faithful" (Heb. 10:23).

The division of theology which focuses on future events is *eschatology*, from the Greek word meaning last, as in the phrase "the last days" (see 2 Tim. 3:1). This is one of the areas in which the difference between covenant theology with its figurative hermeneutic, and dispensational theology with its literal hermeneutic is especially obvious. On the one hand covenant theology tends to view God's promises about future events as allegorical statements. Prophetic passages are understood to teach spiritual truths to the one people of God throughout all of history. Remember our discussion of Isaiah 11:6-9 in chapter one? Covenant theology views passages like this as having spiritual significance for the believer's daily life rather than any literal futuristic meaning. In contrast, because dispensationalism uses a literal hermeneutic, it looks for a time when a literal peace will exist on earth even among the animals. So the two methods come to very different conclusions regarding what the Bible teaches about God's plan for the future.

Specifically, dispensationalism understands the Bible to teach that God has made promises to the nation Israel which He will someday literally fulfill. However, in this present dispensation God's people is the Church, the Body of Christ, and our hope, our future is different from Israel's in some important details. Carefully distinguishing between the two hopes is important if we are to reap the full benefit of Scripture's teachings on the subject. God has graciously provided encouragement to our faith by telling us His plans, but receiving that benefit depends on accurate interpretation. Misinterpreted or misapplied promises may sometimes be worse than no promises at all!

ISRAEL'S AGENDA

Because Israel was God's special people He gave them many unique blessings, as Paul points out in Romans 9:4,5. They were given a land, the law, a priesthood, a temple and its worship system, and the prophets. God also told them of His plans for their future as a nation, and it is a glorious future indeed. The specifics are laid out in a variety of passages, and to discuss them in any detail is beyond the scope of this book. But the basic theme of the prophecies is clear: Israel will one day be the spiritual and political center of the world as the Messiah Himself comes and reigns over the earth from Jerusalem. (Note that the words "Messiah" and "Christ" are synonyms; the first is a Hebrew word and the second is its Greek equivalent.) Christ's second coming will be at a time when Israel is under the fiercest attack of her entire history as a nation. Zechariah writes,

> A day of the LORD is coming when your plunder will be divided among you. I will gather all the nations to Jerusalem to fight against it; the city will be captured, the houses ransacked, and the women raped. Half of the city will go into exile, but the rest of the people will not be taken from the city (Zech. 14:1,2).

Daniel describes it as, "a time of distress such as has not happened from the beginning of nations until then" (Dan. 12:1). In chapter 9, Daniel says this time of persecution will last for one "seven," or a period of seven years (see Dan. 9:27). This period is often called the Tribulation, based on the wording of Revelation 7:14.

At the end of this seven-year period, just when things look hopeless for Israel and the inhabitants of Jerusalem, Messiah will return to earth, fight on behalf of His people Israel, and deliver them from their enemies. Zechariah gives perhaps the most vivid description of that key moment in history.

> Then the LORD will go out and fight against those nations, as he fights in the day of battle. On that day his feet will stand on the Mount of Olives, east of Jerusalem, and the Mount of Olives will be split in two from east to west, forming a great valley, with half of the mountain moving north and half moving south. You will flee by my mountain valley, for it will extend to Azel (Zech. 14:3-5).

The chapter goes on to describe the judgment God will bring upon the nations who have attacked Israel, but the climax of the section is verse 9, "The LORD will be king over the whole earth. On that day there will be one LORD, and his name the only name."

Messiah's coming and His reign from Jerusalem have been Israel's great hope since the earliest stages of her existence as a nation. The specifics of this great future have been revealed progressively through the ministry of Israel's prophets. As early as Deuteronomy 18:18 there is a hint of Christ's role as Israel's greatest prophet when God tells Moses, "I will raise up for them a prophet like you from among their brothers; I will put my words in his mouth, and he will tell them everything I command him." The Davidic covenant in 2 Samuel 7:16 promises David that, "Your house and your kingdom will endure forever before me; your throne will be established forever."

Isaiah, one of Israel's early prophets, has much to say about the Messiah and His reign on earth. In 9:7 we read:

> Of the increase of his government and peace
> there will be no end.
> He will reign on David's throne
> and over his kingdom,
> establishing and upholding it
> with justice and righteousness
> from that time on and forever.
> The zeal of the Lord Almighty
> will accomplish this.

As we have already seen, Isaiah chapter 11 describes in considerable detail the Messiah and His reign. Here we read He will be a descendant of Jesse (David's father), and His kingdom will be characterized by justice and peace as He rules over the earth through a regathered Israel.

Add to these the many prophecies about His coming in the later prophets and it is not surprising Israel developed a very strong messianic hope. The predictions of Jeremiah, Ezekiel, Daniel, and almost all of what we call the "minor prophets" came together to produce in the Jews, especially those living in Palestine, an intense longing for the coming of the Messiah. *They* certainly understood these passages literally. As a result, the Jews anxiously waited for the day the Christ, the Messiah, would come to earth, destroy Israel's enemies, and clearly establish Israel as His special people. He would rule over the earth from David's throne in a restored Jerusalem. Imagine Israel's anticipation at the glory which will be hers! In Zechariah 8:22,23 they read:

> And many peoples and powerful nations will come to Jerusalem to seek the Lord Almighty and to entreat him. This is what the Lord Almighty says: "In those days ten men from all languages and nations will take firm hold of one Jew by the edge of his robe and say, 'Let us go with you, because we have heard that God is with you.'"

By the time the New Testament opened, these messianic hopes had risen to a very high level. Israel and Jerusalem had been under foreign domination, first by the Babylonians, then the Persians, then the Greeks, and finally the brutal Romans. Any Jew with an ego and a little bit of charisma could proclaim himself to be the Messiah and attract a group of followers ready to go to battle, and history tells us there were more than a few such men. But one was unique.

John the Baptist announced: "Repent, for the kingdom of heaven is near" (Matt. 3:2). He explained he was not the Messiah, but was "the voice of one calling in the desert, 'Make straight the way for the Lord'" (John 1:23). When John saw Jesus he pointed Him out as the Lamb of God, the One greater than himself. Andrew, one of the first to follow Jesus, went to his brother Simon Peter and said, "We have found the Messiah" (John 1:41).

Jesus Himself said the kingdom of heaven was near (Matt. 4:17), and at one point asked Peter who Peter thought He was. "Simon Peter answered, 'You are the Christ, the Son of the living God.' Jesus replied, 'Blessed are you, Simon son of Jonah, for this was not revealed to you by man, but by my Father in heaven'" (Matt. 16:16,17). Unlike others who professed to be the Christ, the Messiah, Jesus substantiated His claim by performing miracles. These had the effect of drawing large crowds of hopeful people to Him. "Now while he was in Jerusalem at the Passover Feast, many people saw the miraculous signs he was doing and believed in his name" (John 2:23). This made the Pharisees jealous, and they tried to kill him because of His clear claim to be God in the flesh (see John 5:18 and 10:31-33 as examples).

We can easily imagine why the Twelve remained faithful, even after the crowds had deserted Him. The apostles believed Jesus was the Christ, and that He would bring the promised kingdom to Israel. On the Tuesday before His crucifixion Jesus stood with the Twelve on the Mount of Olives and, looking back at Jerusalem, told them the temple would be destroyed. They asked, "When will this happen, and what will be the sign of your coming and of the end of the age?" (Matt. 24:3). The section which follows, Matthew chapters 24 and 25, is known as the Olivet Discourse, and in it Jesus laid out in considerable detail the events which will precede the establishment of the promised kingdom. He told them about the persecution of the Tribulation and the many false messiahs who will appear. Then, beginning at 24:30, He described the coming of the Son of Man. His coming will be in judgment as the nations of the earth are punished for their wickedness and for their persecution of Israel. Finally, through a series of parables Jesus taught the apostles that the righteous believers of Israel and the Gentile nations will go into the kingdom of God while the wicked are sent away to their judgment. Diagramed as a time line the sequence of events would look like this:

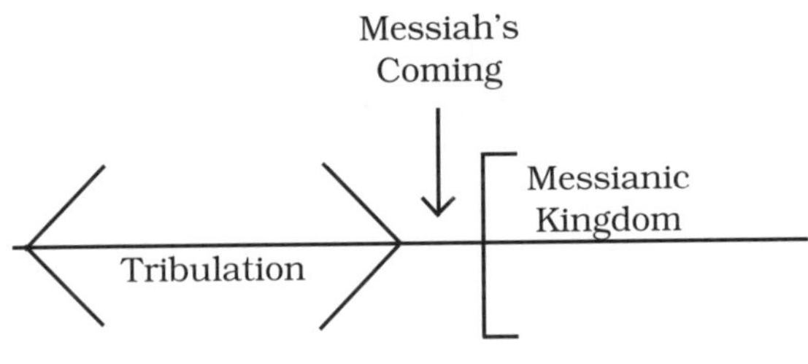

Figure 6.a

This discourse must have filled the Twelve with optimistic excitement. After centuries of national waiting they now stood in the presence of the Messiah and heard Him talk of the kingdom which for three years He had told them was near. But if the Olivet Discourse lifted their hopes, the events of the last half of that week must have crushed them. Like virtually all Jews the Twelve had focused on the prophecies which predicted the Messiah's victorious coming to set up the kingdom. We can understand why those prophecies had caught their imagination and other prophecies had been overlooked. But Isaiah also predicted the Messiah would be despised and rejected by men, be oppressed and afflicted and led like a lamb to the slaughter (Isa. 53). Psalm 22 describes a suffering which never took place in David's personal experience and is a graphic description of death by crucifixion. Even Jesus Himself taught the disciples, "'The Son of Man is going to be betrayed into the hands of men. They will kill him, and after three days he will rise.' But they did not understand what he meant and were afraid to ask him about it" (Mark 9:31,32).

When Christ was arrested the apostles were shocked. Peter went so far as to deny knowing Him. Consider their confusion and despair when the One they believed to be Israel's deliverer was taken prisoner by the Romans and handed over for crucifixion. The sight of Jesus hanging lifeless on that Roman cross must have been shattering for them. They did not understand that before the Messiah could set up a righteous and peaceful kingdom there had to be a basis for that righteousness—He had to die for the sins of the world. Christ told Nicodemus, "Just as Moses lifted up the snake in the desert, so the Son of Man must be lifted up, that everyone who believes in him may have eternal life" (John 3:14,15). In Mark 8:31 we read, "He then began to teach them that the Son of Man must suffer many things and be rejected by the elders, chief priests and teachers of the law, and that he must be killed and after three days rise again." That is why Christ proclaimed the kingdom was *near*; it could not be presented to Israel, and through her to the world, until Christ had made atonement for sin. Because the apostles did not grasp this teaching but focused on His promise of the kingdom, His death devastated them.

The disciples' emotional roller coaster was still not finished. To their amazement He rose on the third day as He had promised. Acts 1:3 indicates it took some convincing before they believed He was really alive, and He spent the next forty days speaking about the kingdom of God. Their hopes for the future rose again, and they asked Him, "Lord, are you at this time going to restore the kingdom to Israel?" (Acts 1:6). Christ did not give them a clear answer, but instead said, "It is not for you to know the times or dates the Father has set by his own authority" (v. 7). This must have made them feel cautiously optimistic.

As soon as Christ said this He was taken up to heaven! By now the disciples must have been once again completely confused and probably very discouraged. Would they ever see the promised kingdom? "Suddenly two men dressed in white stood beside them. 'Men of Galilee,' they said, 'why do you stand here looking into the sky? This same Jesus, who has been taken from you into heaven, will come back in the same way you have seen him go into heaven'" (Acts 1:10,11). It is important to note the prophet Zechariah predicted the Messiah would come to the Mount of Olives when He comes to set up the kingdom. That is the same place the disciples stood as they watched Him ascend and listened to the angels tell of His return. In other words, they now realized there must be *two* comings of Messiah. The first coming or advent was to die for the sins of the world, and the second advent will be to establish the promised kingdom.

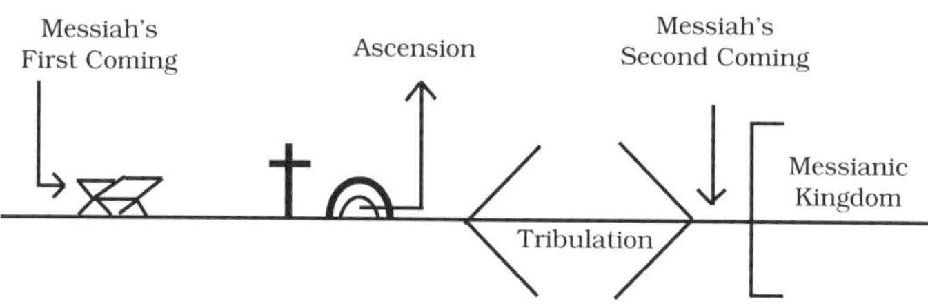

Figure 6.b

How long a period of time would there be between the two comings? Christ gave them no clear indication of the length of time; all they had to go on was His consistent teaching that the kingdom of God was near. But the words and actions of the apostles as recorded in the first few chapters of Acts tell us they expected His return to be very soon, and that they understood it to be conditional.

IMPLICATIONS OF THIS AGENDA

Before we continue our look at those early chapters of Acts we should stop to consider the dispensational significance of the events associated with Christ's first coming. One thing we see is that Christ's ministry took place within the dispensation of Law. He came to Israel, proclaimed Himself to be the promised Christ, the Messiah, and lived a life in complete obedience to the Mosaic Law. To be sure, He did not submit to the legalistic *traditions* of the Pharisees, but the Sermon on the Mount shows us how fully Christ followed the Mosaic Law. He was circumcised as an infant, kept the Sabbath and holy festivals, and worshiped at the synagogue. Over 200 specific prophecies given in the Old Testament were fulfilled through Christ's life and ministry.

Many people assume when they read the New Testament they are past the point when God has Israel as His special people like He did in the Old Testament. But everything about the life of Christ as recorded in the Gospels indicates the dispensation of Law is still in effect throughout this period.

Another fact worth noting is that the crucifixion of Christ is not the failure for the dispensation of Law. You will recall that the test for the dispensation of Law was to obey God fully (Ex. 19:5). In return for their standing as God's special people, Israel is expected to completely obey Him at any time He gives them any instruction. The Old Testament is full of examples of Israel's failures, but in each case God, as Party #1, spares them the judgment they deserve.

This is the case with the crucifixion as well. Throughout His public ministry Israel had refused to accept that Jesus was their Messiah, rejecting Him and His message (see John 8:37,42-47; 10:24-26; 12:37-41). Israel's enthusiastic response to Him at His entry into Jerusalem (Matt. 21:1-11) proved to be insincere, as demonstrated by the crucifixion just five days later. But Christ prayed "Father, forgive them for they do not know what they are doing" (Luke 23:34). Therefore this act of rejection, while still a failure on Israel's part, does not become the dispensational failure which results in judgment. This is why as the book of Acts opens we are still in a period of time when the dispensation of Law is in effect and God's people, Party #2, is still Israel.

CONTINUING TOWARD A CLIMAX

We return now to the early chapters of Acts. After the startling events surrounding the ascension the apostles and other believers returned to Jerusalem. They had been instructed to do so, and to wait for the promised Holy Spirit (Acts 1:4,5). However, another matter had to be addressed. Because of the defection and suicide of Judas a replacement was needed. The Messiah had promised the apostles they would reign on twelve thrones in the kingdom (Matt. 19:28), but they were one apostle short. Through a careful and divinely guided process the group chose Matthias to take over the apostolic ministry left vacant by Judas.

One of the things worth noting about this incident is the indication that the apostles still see themselves and their nation as moving ahead with God's agenda for Israel. The kingdom is coming and there must be twelve apostles in place when Messiah returns to establish it. The text gives no evidence any dispensational change which sets Israel aside is coming.

Acts chapter 2 is an important passage of Scripture in many ways. In our last chapter we saw that the giving of the Holy Spirit as a permanent Indweller for all believers is something which begins here and is connected with the saving work of Christ. It is not connected with any dispensational dynamics. However, many dispensationalists consider Acts 2 to be the beginning of the dispensation of Grace. Those who were saved at this point are considered the first members of the Body of Christ. In order to clarify that issue we should read this and subsequent chapters in Acts and ask some questions. Do the words and events of these chapters fit best with the dispensation of Grace which was a secret until it was revealed by God and in which Jew and Gentile are equal? Or are these chapters consistent with the agenda God had already laid out for Israel, in which she will be the center of a worldwide kingdom established when her Messiah returns to Jerusalem? Again, it is not the purpose of this book to be an exhaustive treatment of this subject or any particular section of Scripture. But a general overview of these early chapters in Acts should serve our purposes well.

For example, note that at Pentecost all those in attendance were either Jews by birth or proselytes to Judaism (Acts 2:5,11). Peter addressed them as such when he spoke to them (vv. 14,22). He very clearly told the crowd the events which they were witnessing were the fulfillment of the prophecy made by Joel about the last days (vv. 16,17). But the clincher is in verse 36 where Peter says, "Therefore let all Israel be assured of this: God has made this Jesus, whom you crucified, both Lord and Christ."

Peter proclaims to the Jews that Jesus was their Christ, their Messiah! What should be Israel's response? They should repent of their sins and be baptized so as to save themselves from "this corrupt generation" (v. 40). Remember, when the Messiah returns He will come in judgment on all who do not believe. In fact many did believe Peter's message, and met regularly in the temple courts (v. 46).

Peter's sermon in chapter three is also helpful in determining which dispensation is in operation in early Acts. After Peter healed the crippled man at the temple a crowd gathered. Once again Peter addressed them as "men of Israel" (3:12). He explained that the man was healed by the name of Jesus whom they had crucified. But this crucifixion was according to the plan of God who had said the Messiah would suffer (v. 18). What should be Israel's response? "Repent, then, and turn to God, so that your sins may be wiped out, that times of refreshing may come from the Lord, and that he may send the Christ, who has been appointed for you—even Jesus" (vv. 18-20).

Once again Peter climaxed his sermon to a gathering of Jews by proclaiming Jesus to be the Christ, the Messiah. And he concluded by declaring, "Indeed, all the prophets from Samuel on, as many as have spoken, have foretold these days. And you are heirs of the prophets and of the covenant God made with your fathers" (vv. 24,25). Israel here stands in a position of unique opportunity. If she will repent and turn back to God after generations of rebellion, He will send Jesus the Christ, the Messiah, to set up the kingdom which had been promised through the prophets. Peter declares that this generation of Jews can inherit the kingdom!

Sadly, the record of the next few chapters is one of Israel's rejection of this offer of the kingdom. Immediately Peter and John were arrested, the first of a string of arrests and beatings. Again, a group of Jews did believe and meet together. But notice where they met—at Solomon's Colonnade at the temple (Acts 5:12). Because of persecution they were forced to pool their resources and help those believers in need. Eventually Stephen was arrested by the Sanhedrin, the Jewish court. He made a speech to them in which he reviewed Israel's history, a history of rejection and persecution of the prophets, which has now climaxed with their crucifixion of the promised Messiah. Yet, Stephen says, they remained stiff-necked, stubborn. As we know, the leaders of Israel responded with fury and stoned Stephen to death. This brought great persecution against the believers.

Everything in these early chapters of Acts is consistent with the dispensation of Law and with God's continuing agenda for Israel which climaxes with the kingdom. The people are Jews, the activity is in Jerusalem, things which take place are the fulfillment of Old Testament prophecies, and the issue at hand is Israel's response to the offer of the kingdom. Will they believe that Jesus whom they crucified was their Christ? If they will, the Messiah will return and the nation will receive the kingdom. But what will happen if they do not?

THE HISTORICAL PARALLEL

Do you remember what happened when God brought Israel out of Egypt? He took them to Sinai where they received the Law and built the tabernacle. From Sinai the nation traveled to Kadesh Barnea on the southern edge of the Promised Land. We read in Numbers 13 that twelve spies were sent into the land from Kadesh Barnea and returned with a report of its splendor. However, ten of the twelve advised the people they had no hope of conquering the land because of the fierce people and fortified cities they saw. Only Joshua and Caleb told the people to trust God and possess the land. The people chose to believe the recommendation of the ten and turned their backs on the land God had prepared for them. As a result God sentenced them to die in the wilderness. Over the next forty years everyone who voted with the ten pessimistic spies died, and a new generation was raised up to receive the land promised to Abraham and his descendants.

A remarkable parallel can be seen between the events recorded in the early chapters of Numbers and those of the early portion of Acts. In each case Israel was offered something promised to her over generations. In each case the nation, under the direction of its leaders, rejects the offer. And in each case God withdrew the offer until a later time. Just as the spies tasted samples of the goodness of the land, so the Jews in Peter's day experienced some of the characteristics of the kingdom: people were miraculously healed, the dead were raised, there was immediate and perfect judgment upon the wicked (Ananias and Sapphira), and other miraculous things which had been predicted about the kingdom age took place (Acts 2:15ff). But as we read in Hebrews 6:4-6,

> It is impossible for those who have once been enlightened, who have tasted the heavenly gift, who have shared in the Holy Spirit, who have tasted the goodness of the word of God and the powers of the coming age, if they fall away, to be brought back to repentance, because to their loss they are crucifying the Son of God all over again and subjecting him to public disgrace.

The early chapters of Acts are the record of the closing days of the dispensation of Law and what should have been the opening days of the dispensation of the Kingdom. Israel stood at the threshold. However, as at Kadesh Barnea, Israel rejected God's offer of the kingdom by refusing to believe Jesus was the Messiah, the Christ. This rejection seems to climax in Acts 7 with the stoning of Stephen by the Sanhedrin.

Here, then, is a key event in Israel's history. After almost 1,500 years of privileged relationship Israel has rejected the offer of the promised kingdom made possible by the first coming and redemptive work of Christ. This is the failure for the dispensation of Law. Because of their rejection God sets Israel aside as His Party #2, and begins a new dispensation, one which was never even hinted at prior to this point.

It is not a coincidence that the account of Stephen's stoning ends with the first mention of Paul, then called Saul. Luke, the author of Acts, is setting the stage for one of the most dramatic and surprising developments in God's plan for human history—the opening of the gospel to all humankind without distinction. This dispensational change was brought about by means of a special revelation given to Paul for all people (Eph. 3:2).

We would expect that with this new dispensation there would also be a new hope, a different agenda for the future. God promised Israel the kingdom, and as Paul reminds us in Romans 11:29, "God's gifts and his call are irrevocable." Just as another generation took possession of the Promised Land, so another generation of Israel will, at some point in the future, receive the kingdom. The book of Revelation makes that clear. But within this dispensation a distinctive and different promise is made to members of the church which is His Body.

CONCLUSION

Because the dispensation of Grace was a mystery, a secret, and because it interrupts the prophetic agenda laid out for Israel, many have visualized it as a parenthetic dispensation. Accordingly, a time line would look something like this:

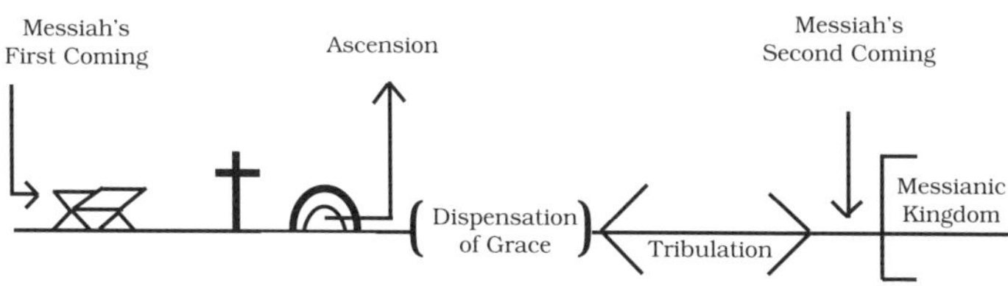

Figure 6.c

How will this dispensation end and what is our hope as members of the Body of Christ? We will look at this issue in our next chapter. But our very limited look at eschatology has already answered some important questions. We have seen that it is not only possible but appropriate to interpret the Old Testament prophecies about the Messiah and His kingdom literally. We have learned that the Gospels and the early chapters of Acts record events which took place within the dispensation of Law. And we have identified the failure for that dispensation as Israel's rejection of Jesus as her promised Messiah and the offer of the kingdom. Our completed dispensational chart is now representated by Figure 6.d.

STUDY QUESTIONS

1. What does the word *eschatology* mean?
2. What event is the focal point for Israel's future?
3. What is the Greek equivalent for the Hebrew word *Messiah*?
4. Why could not Christ set up the kingdom when He came the first time?
5. Why was choosing a replacement for Judas such a high priority?
6. What is the general content of the early chapters of Acts?
7. In what way are the events at Kadesh Barnea a parallel to the events in early Acts?
8. What is the failure for the dispensation of Law?

Name	Innocence	Conscience	Human Gov't	Promise	Law	Grace	Millennial Kingdom
Test	Fill, Subdue, Don't Eat	Obey Conscience	Fill and Subdue	Dwell in Canaan	Obey God Fully	Accept Salvation	Submit to His Reign
Failure	Ate	EVIL!	Gathering at Babel	Moved to Egypt	Rejection of Kingdom	Reject Salvation	Rebel under Satan
Judgment	Cast out, Pain & Toil, Death	Flood	Confusion of Languages	400 Years of Slavery	Set Aside	Tribulation	Destroyed in Battle
Party #2	Adam & Eve	Humankind	Humankind	Abraham and Descendants	Israel	Humankind	Humankind

Figure 6.d

- Chapter 7 -

WE DO NOT WANT YOU TO BE IGNORANT

God's plan for the Body of Christ

The believers in Thessalonica were the kind of people anybody would love. They had eagerly responded to Paul's preaching of the gospel by throwing out their idols and turning to Jesus Christ. Nowhere else had Paul found a group of people, a few Jews and many Gentiles, more ready to receive the good news of salvation through Christ. Yet this very readiness proved to be a problem. It made other Jews in Thessalonica jealous of the large number of converts. As a result they enlisted some thugs from the marketplace to start a riot designed to locate Paul and his helper, Silas, and accuse them of some act of treason. When they could not be located the mob hauled their host, Jason, in front of the city officials and accused him of harboring the traitors. Jason was forced to post bond before his release, while Paul and Silas were kept safely away from the crowd.

As soon as it was dark Paul and Silas were sneaked out of town, just three weeks after their arrival. Unfortunately, this meant leaving behind a group of very young Christians with little knowledge about their new faith. Paul was so concerned about their spiritual well-being that just a few weeks later he sent Timothy back to Thessalonica to strengthen and encourage them. He also wrote them two letters in the subsequent months which we know as 1 and 2 Thessalonians. These are valuable to us because they teach some of the basic truths affecting members of the Body of Christ. What the Thessalonian believers needed to know we also need to understand.

One major concern for those Thessalonian Christians was the status of believers who had died. Apparently, some of their group had died in the few months since Paul had been there, and these young believers were worried about their status. Were those who died before Christ's return left out of the glory which will come with that event? Paul takes up that issue beginning in 1 Thessalonians 4:13 with the words, "Brothers, we do not want you to be ignorant about those who fall asleep, or to grieve like the rest of men, who have no hope." He goes on to outline for them the agenda God has laid out for the Body of Christ. Not surprisingly, it is different in some key aspects from the agenda He has set for Israel. Paul did not want the Thessalonian believers ignorant of God's unique plan for the Body of Christ, and the fact that this material is in the Bible means God does not want us ignorant of it either.

GOD'S AGENDA FOR THE BODY OF CHRIST

Our hope does not focus on the establishment of a messianic kingdom centered in Jerusalem. This passage contains no talk about Messiah's return to the Mount of Olives, His reign on David's throne, or a time of universal peace and righteousness. Paul does not quote any of the great Old Testament passages about the coming messianic age. Instead, in verse 15 of 1 Thessalonians 4 Paul says his source is "the Lord's own word." This is not a reference to Christ's teachings during His earthly ministry, but is instead a reference to the revelation given by God to Paul for this dispensation. As we shall see, the agenda God has for the Body of Christ was a mystery just like all other aspects of the dispensation of Grace. And the mystery was revealed to the apostle Paul.

The first thing Paul tells the Thessalonians is that "God will bring with Jesus those who have fallen asleep in him" (v. 14). This statement teaches us Jesus is coming again, and when He does He will have with Him those of the Body of Christ who have died. This fits with what we read in 2 Corinthians 5:8: "We are confident, I say, and would prefer to be away from the body and at home with the Lord." Members of the Body of Christ who die go to heaven to be with the Lord, and when He returns they will be with Him.

The next thing the Thessalonians learn is that those who are alive when He comes "will certainly not precede those who have fallen asleep" (v. 15). Interpreters are unsure about what Paul means by this statement, but it clearly tells us those who have died are at no disadvantage for having done so. In fact, Paul goes on to say in verse 16 that when the Lord comes down from heaven, the dead in Christ who come with Him "will rise first."

Obviously, the word *rise* here does not refer to the upward direction of travel because they are actually coming down from heaven with the Lord. Yet many Christians are under the wrong impression that deceased believers will get new bodies up from their graves. No, the bodies placed in graves were thoroughly polluted by sin, in most cases are completely decayed, and are of no use in the resurrection. Instead, the word *rise* when used in connection with the subject of resurrection means to get a new body which is sinless and like Christ's glorified body. It comes from the Greek word *anastasis* and literally means *to stand up again*. People who are resurrected get new, glorified physical bodies. Those members of the Body of Christ who have already died at the time He comes will get theirs first, when they come with Him, followed by those who are still living.

The first part of verse 16 together with verse 17 gives us the events associated with this resurrection. His coming will be accompanied "with a loud command, with the voice of the archangel and with the trumpet call of God" (v. 16). As we have seen, the dead in Christ will receive their glorified bodies first, and then, "we who are still alive and are left will be caught up with them in the clouds to meet the Lord in the air" (v. 17). Paul does not explicitly say that living saints get their resurrection bodies at this time, but it does seem to be his meaning. He ends with the statement, "Therefore encourage each other with these words" (v. 18). To know they would be reunited with their brothers and sisters in Christ in the resurrection would encourage the concerned Thessalonians.

This would also fit with what we read in 1 Corinthians 15, the other key passage on future events for the Body of Christ. In verses 51 and 52 of that chapter Paul writes, "We will not all sleep, but we will all be changed—in a flash, in the twinkling of an eye, at the last trumpet. For the trumpet will sound, the dead will be raised imperishable, and we will be changed."

So we learn that at some point in the future Christ will come down from heaven, bringing the physically dead members of the Body of Christ with Him. When this happens they will get their glorified resurrection bodies, then living members of the Body of Christ will be caught up to meet the Lord in the air and receive their new, glorified bodies. From that point onward, "we will be with the Lord forever" (1 Thess. 4:17). This event has been called the *Rapture*, a word which means *to be taken away to a different place*. It is not a word found in the Bible and this has bothered some people, but it accurately describes the event and so serves us well.

In our last chapter we visualized the dispensation of Grace as a parenthetic period which interrupts God's agenda for Israel. The Rapture could be added to that time line with the result looking something like this:

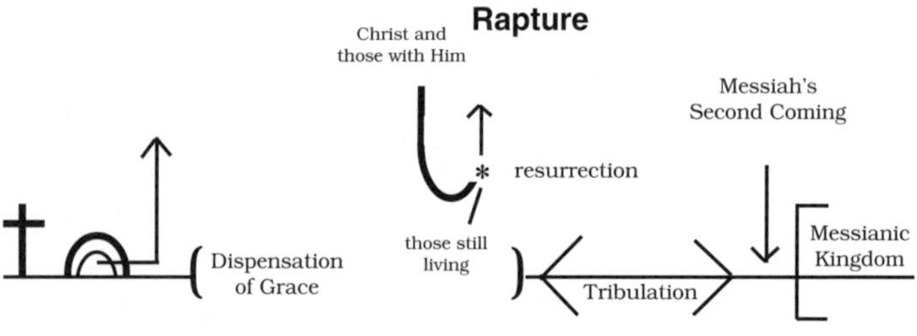

Figure 7.a

SIGNIFICANT DIFFERENCES

Several features of the Rapture show it to be an event entirely different from Christ's Second Coming to set up Israel's kingdom. First, remember that at the Second Coming the Messiah comes to earth, to the Mount of Olives (see Zech. 14:4). He then goes into Jerusalem and sets up the kingdom. But at the Rapture Christ only comes part way to earth and living believers are caught up "in the clouds to meet the Lord in the air" (1 Thess. 4:17). Neither 1 Corinthians 15 nor 1 Thessalonians 4, the two key passages which talk about the Rapture, mention Christ coming to earth.

Secondly, this teaching is given to the Thessalonian Christians because they were worried about their fellow believers who had died, and Paul does not want them to grieve "like the rest of men, who have no hope" (v. 13). Paul closes the section with the words, "Therefore encourage each other with these words" (4:18). That is, the truth of the Lord's coming in the air for the Body of Christ is a comfort to us. This contrasts with the tone of passages which speak about Christ's coming to set up the kingdom. The Olivet Discourse (Matt. 24,25) is a warning which talks about the "distress of those days" (24:29), predicts "the nations of the earth will mourn" (24:30), and cautions the nation of Israel about the judgment which will be associated with His coming. It is also interesting to notice that whereas the Rapture happens "in a flash, in the twinkling of an eye" (1 Cor. 15:52), the second coming of Christ to earth is accompanied by visible changes in the sun, moon, and stars, and the nations of the earth "will see the Son of Man coming on the clouds of the sky, with power and great glory" (Matt. 24:30).

Similarities exist between the two events, and these have caused some to confuse the two events as one. For example, a trumpet call is associated with each (Matt. 24:31 and 1 Cor. 15:52), and both events include a resurrection. At the Rapture members of the Body of Christ receive their glorified bodies, and at the Second Coming the martyrs of the Tribulation (along with Old Testament saints) receive their glorified bodies (Rev. 20:4). But these are just similarities and nothing more.

Others have even seen a similarity where there is a contrast. In Matthew 24:40,41, Christ talks about a time when two people will be together until one is taken and the other left. This sounds a little like the language Paul uses to describe the Rapture, causing some to conclude Christ is talking about the same event. But a closer look at the context shows a clear contrast. In the Matthew passage Christ compares the event He describes to the days of Noah. He says that just like the days before the flood, people will be carrying on with normal activities prior to His return. And just as with the flood, those who are not prepared will be taken away. But notice that with both the flood and Christ's return the people who are taken away are taken in judgment, while those who remain are the faithful who receive blessing. Noah and his family were left on the earth while the wicked were carried away by the flood waters. At Christ's return the faithful will be left on earth to enter the kingdom while those who are unbelievers will be taken away to judgment (see Matt. 25:31ff which describes this). Certainly this is the opposite of the Rapture when believers are taken away from the earth to receive their glorified bodies while those left behind face the terrible period of the Tribulation.

But perhaps the clearest indication the Rapture which Paul talks about is different from the Second Coming is found in 1 Corinthians 15:51. There Paul says, "Listen, I tell you a mystery," and goes on to talk about the events of the Rapture. As we have already seen, the word *mystery* means secret, and thus is something unknown until it is revealed, in this case by God to Paul. The Rapture is the key event in God's agenda for the dispensation of Grace and the Body of Christ. The dispensation of Grace was never prophesied, and so it does not surprise us when Paul describes the climax of this dispensation, the Rapture, as a mystery also. By contrast, the Second Coming is a topic which shows up frequently in Old Testament prophecies and in the teachings of Christ in His earthly ministry (see Zech. 8:3 and Matt. 24,25 as examples).

SOME BENEFITS OF ACCURACY

Distinguishing between the Second Coming and the Rapture will help us properly understand biblical passages which discuss God's plans for the future. It will keep us from taking Israel's agenda and confusing it with ours as members of the Body of Christ. For example, Matthew 24:6 warns of wars and rumors of wars, famines, earthquakes, and tremendous persecution just prior to Christ's coming.

Are these events the prelude to the Rapture? Many have looked at the world scene and concluded that based on this passage the Rapture must be very close. But as we have seen, this portion of Scripture is within the context of God's dealings with Israel under the dispensation of Law, and therefore refers to events leading up to His coming to establish the kingdom. What we observe going on around us is nothing more than normal occurrences in a world affected by sin. The calamities at the time of the Messiah's return to Israel will be far beyond anything human history has witnessed.

Are there any events which precede the Rapture and which indicate it is near? Again, if we ask that question about the Second Coming the answer is yes, because the Old Testament and Gospels contain many passages which describe events leading up to the Messiah's arrival. But Paul gives us no signs to watch for in anticipation of the Rapture. In fact, when Paul talks about the Lord's coming for the Body of Christ he seems to indicate that he expects to be among those caught up, not in the group which has died and gone to heaven. In 1 Thessalonians 4:17 he says, "we who are still alive and are left will be caught up." In 1 Corinthians 15:51 he writes, "We will not all sleep, but we will all be changed." In other words, Paul expected the Rapture at any time, and so should we.

All of this helps us understand one other important truth about the timing of the Rapture—it takes place before the Tribulation. The Bible describes the seven-year Tribulation as a time of trouble and persecution. "There will be a time of distress such as has not happened from the beginning of nations until then" (Dan. 12:1). Christ said that if the period went the full seven years no one would survive it (Matt. 24:22). Much of the book of Revelation describes the Tribulation and its troubles, both natural disasters and the persecutions by Satan's puppet ruler. Zephaniah says it is the day of the Lord's wrath, the day of His anger (Zeph. 2:2,3) as He allows Satan to terrify the earth, and especially the nation Israel. Satan becomes God's instrument of judgment.

But we should not worry about how we will fare should we live long enough to see that time. The Rapture will precede the Tribulation, and all believers, members of the Body of Christ who are alive at that time, will be caught up to be with the Lord. That is one of the reasons Paul tells the Thessalonians they should be encouraged by his teaching. In 1 Thessalonians 5:9, after discussing the Tribulation, he writes, "For God did not appoint us to suffer wrath but to receive salvation through our Lord Jesus Christ."

The Tribulation is a time of God's judgment. It functions as a refining fire, testing the nation Israel to identify those who are truly God's people and should enter the kingdom. The parable of the ten virgins in Matthew 25 is an example of a passage which teaches this. Those who do not receive the mark of the beast or worship him will inherit the promised kingdom, but those who do are taken away to judgment (Matt. 24:38-41).

The Tribulation may also serve as the judgment for the dispensation of Grace. Recall that the test for this dispensation is simply to receive the gift of salvation through Christ. Those who do not accept

Christ as their Savior may remain on earth for the Tribulation (see chapter 3), but those who do are removed from this time of God's wrath by means of the Rapture.

CONCLUSION

The Bible leaves many questions about the Rapture unanswered. Will the rest of the world notice we are missing? Will our earthly bodies be left behind or will they accompany us as we ascend to meet Him and receive our new bodies? Will the resurrection body have the appearance of age, and if so, what age? Will we look to be the age we were when we died, or will everyone look like they are thirty-three?

Despite these unanswered questions we are given much important information about God's plan for the future. As Paul said, this is given so that we might be encouraged and encourage each other. In order to do so we must carefully distinguish between God's agenda for the nation Israel which climaxes with the messianic Kingdom, and His future for the Body of Christ which climaxes with the Rapture. The dispensation of Grace, including the Rapture, was a mystery, a secret, revealed to the apostle Paul. Knowing this will help us understand both what he writes in his letters to the Body of Christ and what the prophets and Christ said to Israel. Then we can rejoice in the promise of a reunion in the clouds and an eternity with Christ!

STUDY QUESTIONS

1. Where are members of the Body of Christ who have already died physically?
2. Describe the events associated with the Rapture.
3. Identify the features which show the Rapture to be a separate event from the Second Coming.
4. With both the Second Coming and the Rapture people are "taken away." Explain why this is a contrast and not a similarity.
5. Give support for saying the Rapture comes before the Tribulation.

- Chapter 8 -

MIRACLES IN DISPENSATIONALISM

Is God still doing them?

When I was in Israel a number of years ago I purchased an oil lamp which dates back to the A.D. 300s. At least that is what the man who sold it to me said. I know very little about things that old and so I was naturally suspicious, but our guide told us the shop was reputable. The shop owner also provided me with a "Certificate of Authenticity," a formal looking document which states the lamp really is from the fourth century. Of course, if the man was dishonest enough to sell me a phony lamp he would not have any problem giving me a worthless certificate to go along with it.

AN IMPORTANT GREEK WORD

The Thessalonian Christians we learned about in our last chapter had another problem besides their concern about fellow Christians who had died. It seems they had received a letter which claimed to be from Paul but was in reality a counterfeit. This letter told them they were in the Tribulation, or Day of the Lord, something they probably found easy to believe because they were being persecuted. But in 2 Thessalonians 2:2 Paul tells them, "not to become easily unsettled or alarmed by some prophecy, report or letter supposed to have come from us, saying that the day of the Lord has already come." He goes on to inform them they do not need to worry about the Tribulation because, among other things, "God chose you to be saved" (v. 13). As we have already seen, members of the Body of Christ are raptured before the beginning of the Tribulation.

Paul normally used a scribe to do the actual writing of the letters which he dictated. But it was also Paul's custom to pen the closing greeting himself. He says in 1 Corinthians 16:21, "I, Paul, write this greeting in my own hand." (See also Col. 4:18.) He does the same thing in 2 Thessalonians but adds, "I, Paul, write this greeting in my own hand, which is the *distinguishing mark* in all my letters. This is how I write" (3:17). Paul here tells them that in the future they should look for his distinctive handwritten greeting at the close of each of his letters. If they do not see it they can be sure the letter is another fake and its teachings untrustworthy.

In this verse the English words "distinguishing mark" are used to translate one Greek word, *saemeion*. It is an important word which means exactly what this verse suggests. A *saemeion* is something a person can see, touch, smell, hear, or taste—something the five senses can perceive—which guarantees the authenticity of the item to which it is attached. Paul's handwritten greeting was something they could see and which guaranteed this letter was authentic. The counterfeit letter they had received lacked this guarantee. In theory the certificate of authenticity I received with my oil lamp was a *saemeion*, because it was meant to guarantee the genuineness of the lamp. My diploma has a raised seal attached to it which I can both see and feel and which guarantees the diploma is authentic. You can probably think of many examples from everyday life of something which assures genuineness, which functions as a *saemeion*. Again, a *saemeion* is something perceivable by the five senses which guarantees the authenticity of the thing to which it is attached.

Some people are more trusting than others and are less likely to require a *saemeion*. That may be good because they are not as cynical as the rest of us. On the other hand, as with the Thessalonians, being too trusting is dangerous if it leads a person to accept things which are not genuine. In that case, requiring a *saemeion* is a good idea. Of course if God says something we ought to accept it as genuine and authoritative simply because it comes from Him.

All of this becomes significant in the light of a statement Paul makes in 1 Corinthians 1:22. He says, "Jews demand miraculous signs and Greeks look for wisdom." Here the word "signs" is the plural form of the Greek word *saemeion*. Paul tells us the Jews require miracles which serve as a means of authentication. Like the old saying about people from Missouri, Jews will not believe it if they do not see it. If the Jews do not see a miracle they will not believe the truth delivered to them from God. This statement about the Jews certainly fits with what we read in John's gospel. Consider the following examples.

> Then the Jews demanded of him "What miraculous sign can you show us to prove your authority to do all this?" (Jn. 2:18).
>
> Now while he was in Jerusalem at the Passover Feast, many people saw the miraculous signs he was doing and believed in his name (Jn. 2:23).
>
> "Unless you people see miraculous signs and wonders," Jesus told him, "you will never believe" (Jn. 4:48).
>
> And a great crowd of people followed him because they saw the miraculous signs he had performed on the sick (Jn. 6:2).
>
> So they asked him, "What miraculous sign then will you give that we may see it and believe you? What will you do?" (Jn. 6:30).

In each of these verses the English word "sign" is the Greek word *saemeion*. We see here the outworking of what Paul says in 1 Corinthians 1:22. It is not enough for God to merely say something to the Jews; if they do not have a miracle attached to the message they generally will not believe the message. Christ proclaimed Himself to be the Messiah, but they would not believe His message unless they saw Him do miracles to authenticate His claim.

TWO KINDS OF MIRACLES

The miracles in the Bible can be divided into two categories. First are what we may call *direct miracles*, where God Himself does something outside the laws of nature without using any other agency. The turning of Lot's wife into a pillar of salt would fit into this category, as would the flood, and Sarah bearing a son in her old age. The Bible also records *indirect miracles*. These events are also God's work outside the laws of nature, but in this case He uses someone as an agent through whom He does the miracle. Moses brought forth water from the rock, Elijah raised the widow's son from the dead, and Peter healed a man born lame. Even as we say this we recognize it was God who did the miracle, but He did it through the agency of an individual. These two types of miracles could be diagrammed.

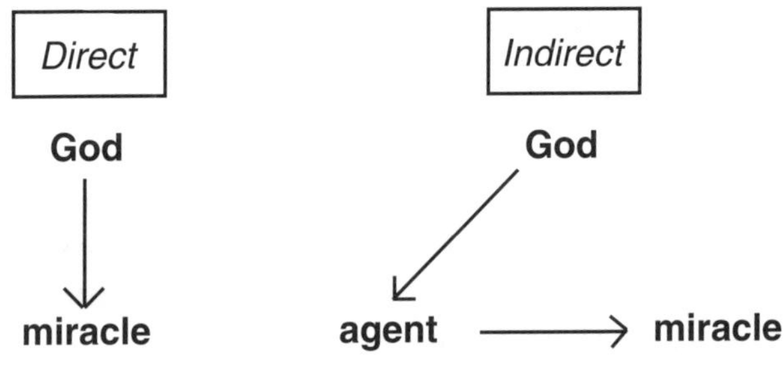

Figure 8.a

The miracles which Christ performed during His earthly ministry are best classified as indirect. Certainly He was God in the flesh, and in that sense they were direct. But all Christ's actions were "the will of him who sent me" (Jn. 6:38), and because He was performing miracles as a part of His Father's commission they should be put in the indirect category.

Why would God do indirect miracles? What purpose is served by doing the supernatural through a human agent instead of directly? The indirect miracle serves as a *saemeion*, authenticating the message of the individual who does it. This is made clear by the answer to another question. Where in Scripture is the first recorded indirect miracle? Interestingly, it is with Moses. After forty years as Pharaoh's son and another forty as a shepherd in the wilderness, the Lord appeared to Moses through a bush which burned but was not consumed (a direct miracle). God told Moses he was to return to Egypt and announce to the Jews that God had called him to lead the Jews out of slavery and into the land promised to their forefathers. Moses asked a very realistic question: "What if they do not believe me or listen to me and say, 'The Lord did not appear to you'?" (Ex. 4:1). Moses knew the character of his people. He knew they would not believe he had been sent by God to deliver them.

The Lord then did something very significant. He first had Moses throw his staff on the ground where it turned into a snake. When Moses picked it up again it returned to being a staff. Next, Moses was instructed to put his hand inside his cloak. He did so, and when he pulled it out it was covered with leprosy. When Moses repeated the procedure his hand was restored to its normal condition. Notice what God says next. "If they do not believe you or pay attention to the first miraculous *sign*, they may believe the second. But if they do not believe these two *signs* or listen to you, take some water from the Nile and pour it on the dry ground. The water you take from the river will become blood on the ground" (Ex. 4:8,9). Moses is given three miracles, *saemeion*, which will serve as signs, proving he has genuinely been sent by God.

God begins His dealings with Israel as His special people in the book of Exodus. Until this time He has dealt either with humankind as a whole (the first three dispensations) or the family of Abraham (the fourth dispensation). But now God begins dealing with Israel as a nation, and He does so through the leadership of Moses. Paul told us the Jews require miraculous signs, and sure enough, just as soon as God starts His unique relationship with Israel we see Him using miraculous signs as a method. The two begin at the same time.

An indirect miracle is a *saemeion*, a sign. It is something which can be observed by the five senses and which authenticates the thing to which it is attached. Moses was the first of many men to bring a message from God to the nation of Israel, but true to Paul's statement in 1 Corinthians 1:22 the Jews will not believe that message unless they see a miracle which serves as a sign, a means of authentication. Both Moses and God knew that, and so Moses was given three miracles to perform which would serve as authentication. No indirect miracles had occurred up until Moses because none were needed. God was not yet dealing with the people who require them, namely Israel. But as soon as He did begin dealing with Israel, indirect miracles became a major part of His methodology.

Notice that when a miracle was done for the purpose of authentication the miracle was not, in and of itself, the important part of what was taking place. The significant thing was the message which Moses was to take to Israel, that he was to lead them out of Egypt. The three miracles served only a supporting role. That was true whether it was Aaron's staff budding, Joshua causing the sun to stand still, or Elijah calling down fire from heaven. The miracles which Christ did while on earth were not simply for the sake of doing miracles but to prove He was who He claimed to be—the Messiah. Notice what Peter says on the day of Pentecost: "Jesus of Nazareth was a man accredited by God to you by miracles, wonders and signs" (Acts 2:22). Peter himself healed the man born lame, as recorded in Acts 3. But this miracle was not primarily for the benefit of that man; it was done so that Peter's sermon which followed would have credibility among the Jews who heard it. Without the miracles they would not have paid Peter a moment's notice. Indirect miracles serve as signs and are secondary to the message to which they are attached.

ONLY ONE TODAY

At this point we are prepared to answer the question, is God doing miracles today? The answer is a qualified yes. We have absolutely no reason to believe God is not still doing direct miracles. They have been a part of His work from the beginning, and undoubtedly continue. These direct miracles may often come in response to the prayers of God's people. Too many dispensationalists have wrongly concluded God is no longer doing miracles and therefore they do not pray for the miraculous. James says, "You do not have, because you do not ask God" (James 4:2).

Indirect miracles, however, were a part of God's methodology for dealing with Israel. As a people Israel required miraculous signs, and so God graciously met that need. When God set aside His special relationship with Israel He also set aside the methodology designed for them. Therefore, God is not doing miracles today through human agents. The distinction is subtle but important. Often in Christian circles today we hear someone disclaiming any personal credit for performing miracles. It is, they say, the work of God. Moses would certainly have said the same thing. But if an individual, either by their words or their actions, puts themselves in the position of being the agent through whom God performs a miracle they assume a role which is not functional in this dispensation. It is not a matter of whether God *could* do indirect miracles in this dispensation; certainly God is capable of anything which does not violate His holy character. The question is whether God *is* doing indirect miracles. And as we have seen, indirect miracles had a dispensational application, and are therefore not part of God's methodology in the dispensation of Grace. In chapter 10 we will discuss Paul's use of indirect miracles in the book of Acts.

"YES, BUT WHAT ABOUT . . . ?"

It is to be expected that someone new to these concepts will have a question at this point. If God is no longer doing miracles through individuals, how do we explain what seems to be evidence to the contrary? That is a fair question which deserves an answer. But another issue should be addressed first.

Which will have priority for the Christian, the Bible or experience? Will Scripture be the judge of our experience or will experience be the judge of Scripture? If the Bible teaches me one thing and my experience seems to say something different I have to choose which will have priority and carry the weight of truth. Unfortunately, in our age experience often wins out. But magicians have encouraged me to stick with the Bible.

I have always found magic acts both entertaining and frustrating. On the one hand I am fascinated by the things the magician does, but I also get inwardly irritated that he or she has put one over on me. They have done something which I know to be impossible, yet I have seen them do it with my own eyes. People are cut in half and then restored, knives are driven through people without any effect, and assistants float in mid-air. Of course, it is all a combination of sleight of hand and clever deception.

The magician learns enough about human thought and behavior patterns to know how to effectively fool us into believing the impossible has taken place. We *see* the assistant floating in air, but we *know* from what we have learned it is not possible. No normal person goes home from the magic show and tells his wife to lie on the kitchen table while he pulls it out from under her. Instead we accept the fact that our five senses are not always trustworthy, and what we *know* to be true has to take priority over what *appeared* to take place.

The same is true in the field of theology. The Bible must be the final court of appeal when it comes to matters of truth. If the Bible says one thing and my experience seems to indicate something else, I must look for another explanation of my experience, not another explanation of Scripture's clear teaching. In this case, if the Bible says the Jews require miraculous signs (indirect miracles) and God has set aside His dealings with the Jews as His special people, then I must look for another explanation of what *seem* to be indirect miracles.

One answer for what appear to be miracles is the same as for the magician's act; that is, both are deception. I do not take offense at the magician for deceiving me; we all accept it as part of the entertainment package. But we hesitate to think someone who claims to be a servant of God would intentionally deceive His people into thinking a miracle had taken place when it was really nothing more than sophisticated trickery. Yet there are enough documented examples, and people who have confessed to being involved, that we cannot deny it is a very real part of the religious landscape. A great deal of money can be made in the name of Christianity, and a few well-placed "miracles" can go a long way toward loosening the purse strings of the faithful.

However, the majority of what appear to be indirect miracles are probably not in the category of deception. Their answers lie in the nature of the illnesses. People in the medical profession tell us that between 50% and 75% of the hospital beds in our country are occupied by people whose symptoms stem from psychosomatic causes. While their symptoms are very real, and sometimes very painful, the primary cause is not some physical disorder but rather a psychological dysfunction. Most of us have had headaches or backaches which we know stem from tension. Emotional distress can cause digestive failure, heart trouble, and in extreme cases things as serious as hallucinations. At least a temporary cure for these physical symptoms can be achieved if a psychological motivation is put in place which is stronger than the one which has caused the symptoms. This motivation may readily come in the form of a desire to experience God's power and healing touch and the affirmation of the crowd of witnesses in attendance.

Still other diseases which are frequently "healed" at religious services are vague, undefined illnesses. Have you ever noticed the absence of the types of indirect miracles which were done during the time of God's relationship with Israel? We do not see the people born blind receiving sight, or the dead being raised. The hungry are not fed from a few morsels of food and devastating storms are not stilled.

Notice again the purpose of the indirect miracles in Scripture. They were not done for their value as miracles in and of themselves. They were attached to something, typically for the purpose of authenticating for the Jews the message of God's servant. They each functioned as a *saemeion*. This contrasts with the healing services of today where the supposed miracle is the central event. And in the Bible the one doing a healing miracle was never ineffective because of a lack of faith on the part of the recipient.

THE MATTER OF TONGUES

At this point we can look at another phenomenon which plays an important role in the lives of many Christians. Speaking in tongues is a key element in a part of Christianity which is sometimes called the charismatic movement. When an individual speaks in tongues they utter a series of sounds which are not understandable to others but which, it is said, are a heavenly language used to praise God. This is viewed as a miraculous manifestation of the indwelling Holy Spirit. The practice is based wrongly on the pattern in Acts 2 when Peter and the disciples spoke in tongues. Is it part of God's program for the Body of Christ?

The first thing to notice about this topic is that the primary passage for speaking in tongues, Acts 2, comes from a period of time within the dispensation of Law. That does not in and of itself mean that speaking in tongues is not a part of this dispensation because it may be a horizontal truth, but it alerts us to the need for careful study.

The next thing is to look carefully at the text of Acts 2 in order to accurately define the miracle known as speaking in tongues. When we do that we discover the miracle of Pentecost was very different from what takes place in churches today. Acts 2:5 tells us, "There were staying in Jerusalem God-fearing Jews from every nation under heaven." The feast of Pentecost was one of three annual festivals which the Old Testament said should be celebrated in Jerusalem, so Jews had traveled from their homes all over the Mediterranean world to spend the feast day in that city. When they came they found themselves in a city where Aramaic, a variation of Hebrew, was spoken. But on the morning of the feast these people heard a group of Galileans speaking in the languages of their home countries, something which amazed them. The text gives a listing of some of the people present at that gathering, including Medes, visitors from Rome "(both Jews and converts to Judaism)," Cretans and Arabs. Note that these are all Jews. They are called Arabs, for example, in the same sense I am called an American—it is the country of my birth. My ethnic heritage is mostly Scandinavian, and these individuals are Jews. No Gentiles were present at Pentecost, which is why in verse 14 Peter addresses them as "fellow Jews."

The miracle of Pentecost was that these Jews from all over the empire heard the Galilean disciples "declaring the wonders of God in our own tongues" (v. 11). The disciples were miraculously able to speak real, existing languages which they themselves had no way of knowing. Many versions use the words "other tongues" to translate the Greek words used here. For example, in verse 4 it says, "All of them were filled with the Holy Spirit and began to speak in other tongues as the Spirit enabled them." That is an appropriate translation because it is the literal meaning of the Greek words in the text. But the context tells us the word *tongues* is here being used in the same sense we do when we use the expression "mother tongue." It is the equivalent of the word *language*. No reasonable way can be found to understand the phenomenon of Acts 2 as referring to a new, unknown heavenly language.

All of this leads us to some important conclusions. First, what takes place in churches today is not the equivalent of what took place at Pentecost. When the disciples spoke in tongues they were speaking real, existing languages unknown to them, whereas in today's churches it is a "heavenly language." Secondly, the miracle of Pentecost was for Jews and was an indirect miracle. It was intended not to stand by itself but to serve as authentication for the message of Peter and the apostles as they went on to proclaim Jesus as Israel's Messiah. Thirdly, this event was the fulfillment of a prophecy made through Joel, as Peter says in verse 16.

This is consistent with Paul's instruction in 1 Corinthians 14:22 where he says, "Tongues, then, are a sign [*saemeion*], not for believers but for unbelievers." Some Bible students read Paul's discussion on tongues in 1 Corinthians 12-14 and conclude that the term here means something other than an existing language as it does in Acts 2, but the Greek words are exactly the same in both passages and it is best to understand the meaning as the same. But whatever the meaning of the word "tongues" in 1 Corinthians it is clear what Paul says about it. Paul calls tongues a *saemeion* intended not for believers but for unbelievers, and in chapter 1:22 he told us Jews require signs. That seems to exclude the sign gift of tongues from God's order for the dispensation of Grace.

Once again the question is asked, if it is not a part of God's order how do we explain what is taking place today? And once again we are faced with the decision regarding priorities. Will our experience judge Scripture or will Scripture judge our experience? It is also interesting to note that what is called "ecstatic speech" is not unique to certain segments of Christianity. The practice of speaking in unintelligible sounds is common in many primitive religions and in some eastern religions. Mormonism identifies it as one of the elements of their articles of faith. It is a psychological phenomenon and a learned behavior, not a miracle like that which took place at Pentecost.

CONCLUSION

It can seem harsh and judgmental to criticize the practices of brothers and sisters in Christ. Most of those who believe in indirect miracles such as healings and in "speaking in tongues" are sincere Christians who desire God's fullest blessing in their lives. Some have made tongues (here we mean ecstatic speech, not the miracle of Acts 2) a measure of spirituality, suggesting believers who have not had the experience have not completely yielded to the Holy Spirit. But many would make no such demand on others. They only desire the experience as part of their relationship with God.

Here we must say it is not our goal to judge other members of the Body of Christ. Our desire is to accurately understand the Word of God and to conform to His will for us in this dispensation. In 2 Timothy 2:15 Paul told Timothy, "Do your best to present yourself to God as one approved, a workman who does not need to be ashamed and who correctly handles the word of truth." This correct handling includes distinguishing between horizontal and vertical truths. Our aim is personal, not directed at others. It is that we should be correct handlers of the word of truth.

The sure way to fullest blessing in the Christian life is complete conformity to the Word of God. Anything else may provide a temporary lift, but in the long run if it is not in accord with the Bible it cannot serve to strengthen my walk with Him. It may, in fact, cause me to focus attention on my experience instead of biblical truth. Sooner or later my experiences will fail me and when that happens my walk with God will suffer.

God is still a God of miracles. He continues to do wonderful things which defy natural explanation, and the attentive Christian praises Him for these miracles. But the indirect miracles which were part of His relationship with Israel were set aside with that relationship and are no longer functional in this dispensation. To recognize that does not diminish God, but instead increases our potential for experiencing the unique blessings which are ours in the dispensation of Grace.

STUDY QUESTIONS

1. What does the word *saemeion* mean?
2. What does Paul say about the Jews in 1 Corinthians 1:22? Explain what he means.
3. Describe the two kinds of miracles in the Bible.
4. Is God still doing miracles today? Explain your answer.
5. What was the biblical miracle of tongues?
6. What does Paul say about tongues in 1 Corinthians 14:22?

- *Chapter 9* -

WATER BAPTISM

Sorting out teaching and tradition

Do psychiatrists really have patients lie on a couch and respond to individual words, or is free association something they created for psychiatrists on television shows? Whatever the answer, the method may prove to be a helpful way to begin our look at the somewhat controversial topic of baptism. You will not get a bill for $70.00 when it is over, and you will not be able to close your eyes and relax as we do this because you are reading and not listening. Nonetheless, think of the first word which comes to mind when you read:

Computer
Home
Banana
Baptism

I have tried this little exercise with hundreds of people over the years and the vast majority have the same response when they hear the word *baptism*. Most of them respond with the word *water*.

Did you? If you did, it is not surprising because the word baptism is almost always used in connection with the religious ceremony which involves water. Various denominations have different views on the subject of water baptism. Some baptize infants and some baptize only adults. Some sprinkle the water, some pour it, and some immerse the individual completely. In some denominations baptism is entirely optional while others make it a requirement of church membership and still others believe it is necessary for salvation. But most Christians have never questioned whether it is a part of what we should do, whatever form it may take.

Much of the confusion about water baptism stems from this association of the words *water* and *baptism*, and the unconscious tendency to think the two are always connected. If you remember your grammar well enough you may be able to recall that in a term like *water baptism* the first word functions as an adjective and describes the second word, the noun *baptism*. This suggests there may be other kinds of baptism and other adjectives which could go in front of the word. As it turns out that is exactly the case. The Bible mentions a number of baptisms, many of which have nothing to do with water.

What is the basic meaning of the word baptism? A survey of the different ways the word is used in Scripture will go a long way in getting to its basic meaning. For example, Matthew 3:11 mentions three different kinds of baptism in one verse. John the Baptist told the people, "I baptize you with water for repentance. But after me will come one who is more powerful than I, whose sandals I am not fit to carry. He will baptize you with the Holy Spirit and with fire." Of the three baptisms mentioned in this verse one involves water, one the Holy Spirit, and one fire. These are very different from each other. In Luke 12:50 Christ says, "But I have a baptism to undergo, and how distressed I am until it is completed!" He spoke these words almost three years after John had baptized Him with water, a baptism which certainly did not cause Him to be distressed. Christ is here using the word baptism to refer to His approaching death.

Another passage which illustrates that the word baptism does not have water as a basic part of its meaning is 1 Corinthians 10:2. Here Paul is telling us some of the lessons we should learn from Israel's history. In describing the nation he says, "They were all baptized into Moses in the cloud and in the sea." One thing which is clear about Israel's exodus from Egypt is that they passed through the sea without getting wet! If anyone was baptized with water in that event it was the Egyptian army, and they were immersed. But Paul says Israel was baptized into Moses, not water.

The word baptism is a noun, and as we have seen, the adjectives used with it include water, the Holy Spirit, fire, death, and Moses. What is the common characteristic which makes each of these adjectives fit with the word baptism? A *change* is described in each case. With the exception of water, which we will discuss more thoroughly in a bit, these adjectives each describe a change which is both complete and lasting. A baptism is anything which produces a complete and permanent change in the object being baptized. The Holy Spirit, fire, and death are obviously complete and permanent changes, and so each qualifies as a baptism. When Israel left Egypt under Moses' leadership they went from being a family group of nearly three million people to being a nation, a change which has had and will have a tremendous effect on human history.

This fits with the way the word baptism was used in everyday speech during New Testament times. It was not exclusively a religious term. For example, in the first century the word baptism was used to describe dyeing fabric, which is consistent with what we have learned about the basic meaning of the word, because dyeing fabric brings about a complete and permanent change.

We are creatures of habit, to be sure. But no matter how hard it may be, we need to re-educate ourselves when it comes to the word baptism. When we hear or read the word we must first think not about water, but of a change which is thorough and lasting.

WHERE DID WATER BAPTISM COME FROM?

Another part of our retraining is understanding the origin of the baptisms which do involve water. The noun form of the Greek word is *baptismos* and the verb form is *baptidzo*. This similarity to our English word group shows us our word baptism is not a translation of the Greek word. A translation gives the equivalent meaning in another language. For example, the Spanish word *casa*, when translated into English, becomes the word *house*, which has the same meaning. Our word baptism is a transliteration. A transliteration merely takes the letters and sounds of a word in one language, in this case the Greek word *baptismos*, and transfers them into their equivalent letters and sounds in another language. But a transliteration does not convey the meaning of a word. This explains why our word baptism does not convey the sense of a complete and permanent change.

It also explains why the English word baptism never occurs in the Old Testament. The Old Testament was written in Hebrew and our word baptism is a transliteration of a Greek word. So when the Old Testament is translated from Hebrew into English no transliterations of Greek words are seen. But because most Christians do not realize this little piece of language trivia, they assume baptism (and most people here think about water baptism) is a New Testament truth. After all, they never read the word baptism in the Old Testament. However, the Old Testament is full of baptisms which are described with Hebrew words. These are then translated into English with words other than baptism. The most common English words used in the Old Testament are *dip* and *wash*.

Various water baptisms were a key element in the Jewish ritual system. The tabernacle structure included a water basin where priests daily washed themselves in a ceremony which was to precede any other activities (Ex. 30:17-21). If an article such as a garment or pitcher came in contact with an unclean animal which had died, that article was to be ceremonially cleansed by putting it in water (Lev. 11:32).

This ritual of water baptism was so much a part of Jewish life that Mark tells us the Pharisees had added baptisms to those required by the Mosaic Law. He says,

> The Pharisees and all the Jews do not eat unless they give their hands a ceremonial washing, holding to the tradition of the elders. When they come from the marketplace they do not eat unless they wash. And they observe many other traditions, such as the washing of cups, pitchers and kettles (Mark 7:3,4).

In these verses the English words "wash" and "washing" are translations of the original Greek word *baptidzo*.

Have you ever wondered why the people, especially the Pharisees, were not absolutely befuddled to see John baptizing Jews in the Jordan River? If they had never seen anything like it before, it certainly would have struck them as a very strange thing to do. But the Pharisees did not ask, "What are you doing?" They asked John, "Why do you baptize?" The reason for this question was that they were very familiar with the ceremony itself because water baptism was a basic Jewish ceremony. But they could not understand why John was performing it on Jews.

About 200 years before Christ was born the Jewish rabbis were concerned that very few Jews outside of Palestine were reading and studying the Scriptures. The everyday language of the empire was Greek, and what we now call the Old Testament was in Hebrew, a foreign language to Jews of the dispersion. They were not studying their Scriptures because they could not read them. So in the

Egyptian city of Alexandria a group of Jewish scholars (tradition says there were seventy of them) set about to translate the Hebrew Scriptures into Greek. This great effort resulted in what we now call the Septuagint. The Septuagint is normally referred to by the symbol LXX, the Roman numeral designation for seventy, thus commemorating the seventy scholars who worked on the project. The LXX is the translation of the Hebrew Old Testament into Greek, done about 200 years before Christ.

What is interesting is that these Jewish scholars used the Greek word *baptismos* in its various forms twenty-two times as they did their translation. Clearly they thought the concept associated with the word baptism was present in the Old Testament. In some passages the word baptism was used to describe a particular religious ceremony, as it is in Leviticus 4:6 and 17 where the priest is to "dip" his finger in the blood of the sacrifice. In Leviticus 11:32 instructions are given about ceremonially unclean articles which should be "put in" water. Other times the word baptism in the LXX has a non-religious meaning as it does in Ruth 2:14 where Boaz invites Ruth to "dip" her bread in the wine vinegar. But the concept of baptism, including water baptism in religious ceremonies, is not something which appears for the first time in Matthew.

Water baptism was an important part of the Mosaic Law and its religious system. It is still a Jewish ritual. This is clear when one looks at the practices of orthodox Judaism today. The synagogue of an orthodox Jewish congregation will include a small room which contains what they call a *mikveh*.

If you saw it you would think it looked very much like the baptistry at a typical Baptist church, except at the synagogue it is a separate room. Here the Jewish men and women of the congregation immerse themselves at various times and for various reasons in accordance with the commandments of the Mosaic Law and centuries of Jewish tradition.

It surprises many Christians to learn that orthodox synagogues contain the equivalent of a baptistry. But it is even more of a puzzle to the orthodox Jew that many Christian churches have a *mikveh*, because the Jew knows ceremonial immersion to be a Jewish ritual.

WATER BAPTISM AS CEREMONY

Before continuing it might be helpful to review the two key things we have learned so far. First, we have seen that the basic meaning of the word baptism is to produce a complete and permanent change in the object being baptized. Secondly, water baptism is a Jewish ceremony which has its beginnings in the Mosaic Law and its ritual system.

But these two pieces of information do not seem to go together well. The phrase "a complete and permanent change" is clearly accurate for any baptism involving fire, the Holy Spirit, and death. But what about water or, in the case of some Old Testament baptisms, blood? Getting dipped in water or blood does not produce a change that is complete nor permanent, so how can it be a baptism?

The key to answering this question is the word *ceremony*. In Hebrews 9 the author discusses the worship forms which were used in the Old Testament tabernacle. After describing the structure and some of the ceremonies he says, "This is an illustration for the present time, indicating that the gifts and sacrifices being offered were not able to clear the conscience of the worshiper. They are only a matter of food and drink and various ceremonial washings [*baptismos*]—external regulations applying until the time of the new order" (vv. 9,10).

The Jewish system was full of ceremonies which were significant not because of what they themselves accomplished but because of what they represented. They portrayed a spiritual truth in the form of an outward ritual. In most cases this truth was something which was primarily future and found fulfillment in the work of Christ. For example, the ceremonies associated with Passover commemorated Israel's escape from Egypt, but more significantly they prophetically portrayed Christ's substitutionary death on the cross. The high priest's entrance into the Holy of Holies on the annual Day of Atonement prefigured Christ's offering of His blood as payment for our sins. But as the writer of Hebrews says, these were all "external regulations applying until the time of the new order." They were not effective in and of themselves; they were "not able to clear the conscience of the worshiper."

Paul says the same thing in Colossians when he argues against allowing anyone to force his readers into observing Jewish ceremonies. He says, "Therefore do not let anyone judge you by what you eat or drink, or with regard to a religious festival, a New

Moon celebration or a Sabbath day. These are a shadow of the things that were to come; the reality, however, is found in Christ" (Col. 2:16,17).

Water baptism was (and still is) a Jewish ceremony. It did not effect a complete and permanent change. Its function was to portray to Israel through the symbolism of ritual a spiritual truth about a real and permanent baptism, one which would find its fulfillment in the work of Christ and its implications. What is this baptism which the Old Testament water baptisms foreshadowed?

In Romans 6 Paul writes to believers about their obligation to live holy lives. He says, "Or don't you know that all of us who were baptized into Christ Jesus were baptized into his death? We were therefore buried with him through baptism into death in order that, just as Christ was raised from the dead through the glory of the Father, we too may live a new life" (vv. 3,4). Some people have seen in these words a symbolism which makes the act of immersion into water a parallel to Christ's burial and the coming up out of the water a parallel to His resurrection. But nowhere in the Old Testament is the action of water baptism even remotely connected with the movements of burial and resurrection. The water was always associated with cleansing, and in a majority of the cases it involved dipping or pouring, not immersion. Even most Baptist scholars recognize that here in Romans 6 Paul is not talking about any ritual water baptism but about the same baptism Christ referred to when He used the word to describe His death in Luke 12:50.

As Christians we have been crucified with Christ (Rom. 6:8); we have died with Him. Paul explains that through this death "our old self was crucified with him so that the body of sin might be rendered powerless, that we should no longer be slaves to sin—because anyone who has died has been freed from sin" (Rom 6:6,7). The Old Testament baptism ceremonies "were not able to clear the conscience of the worshiper" (Heb. 9:9,10), but the death of Christ, His baptism of death, has cleansed us. So in Romans 6 Paul urges us to live as a clean people. Because we have been baptized into Christ and His death (a complete and permanent change) we should not live in sin any longer but in the newness of resurrection life. The Old Testament water baptisms foreshadowed the real inward cleansing which is accomplished through the baptism of Christ's death and our participation in that event. No reason exists to go back and duplicate the symbol now that the reality has been realized through Christ's baptism of death.

Scripture does tell us about a baptism which is still being carried out today. In Ephesians 4:4-6 Paul says, "There is one body and one Spirit—just as you were called to one hope when you were called—one Lord, one faith, one baptism; one God and Father of all, who is over all and through all and in all." At first it seems odd for Paul to say there is only one baptism when we have already read about a number of different baptisms in the Bible. Certainly Paul knew his theology well enough to know about the baptisms of fire, death, the Holy Spirit, and Moses.

Paul is saying that at this point in time, in this dispensation, only one baptism is a part of God's ongoing program for the Body of Christ. The baptism he referred to in Romans 6, the baptism of Christ's death, is an accomplished fact and is no longer taking place. But another baptism is taking place on a daily basis. In 1 Corinthians 12:13 Paul writes, "For we were all baptized by one Spirit into one body—whether Jews or Greeks, slave or free—and we were all given the one Spirit to drink." The instant a person accepts Christ as Savior the Holy Spirit baptizes him or her into the Body of Christ. Whether one is Jew or Gentile, in this dispensation of Grace the individual is placed in the Body at the moment of conversion. This clearly qualifies under the definition of baptism because it effects a complete and permanent change. This is the one baptism Paul refers to in Ephesians 4:5.

A CLOSER LOOK AT KEY PASSAGES

If what we have been covering in this chapter is new to you the implications of our discussion are probably apparent. What we have said so far leads to the conclusion that the ritual of water baptism has no place in this dispensation. This comes as a shock to most people who have grown up with water baptism as a part of the Christian church's life. They are astonished at the thought that a practice which has played such a major role in the church could be unbiblical. After all, the Bible refers to it so frequently, and so many passages tell us to be baptized in water. But is this really the case?

The first place most people turn in their effort to support the practice of water baptism is the baptism of Christ by John. The implication is that because Christ was baptized with water and we are to be followers of Christ, we too should be baptized with water. Of course, Christ was also circumcised on the eighth day, kept the Sabbath and worshiped at the temple, but those matters are not viewed as binding on believers today.

When we look at the record of Christ's baptism we learn that John was very reluctant to perform it because he viewed himself as unworthy. But Christ told John, "Let it be so now; it is proper for us to do this to fulfill all righteousness" (Matt. 3:15). What did Christ mean by this statement?

Theologians have long recognized that Christ has three major offices: prophet, priest, and king. (His office of high priest is a key topic in the book of Hebrews.) In the Old Testament we read God's instructions to Israel about who may serve Him as a priest. Those who served in the various priestly functions began their ministry at the age of thirty (Num. 4:46,47). But before they could begin their work as priests they were required to go through what we might call an ordination ceremony. The first time this took place was with Aaron and his sons, and it was to serve as a pattern for succeeding generations. The record of this induction ceremony is in Exodus 29, and it gives us some interesting information. We learn that a set of sacrifices was made to atone for the sins of Aaron and his sons. "Then bring Aaron and his sons to the entrance to the tent of Meeting and wash them with water" (Ex. 29:4). This was then followed by an anointing with oil.

The parallels to the baptism of Christ are striking. He was thirty years old when He came to John for baptizing and this is the event which marks the beginning of His public ministry. Christ had no sin so a sacrifice was not necessary, but He does tell John that a water baptism is necessary "to fulfill all righteousness." Immediately after Christ's baptism the Holy Spirit descends upon Him.

Christ's baptism by John was His ordination ceremony, required by Mosaic Law before He could begin His ministry as our great high priest. Nowhere does Christ or any New Testament writer tell us we are to follow His example in baptism because none of us are in a parallel role.

The next passage typically used as a basis for practicing water baptism is Matthew 28:19,20 which is often called the Great Commission. The passage reads, "Therefore go and make disciples of all nations, baptizing them in the name of the Father and of the Son and of the Holy Spirit, and teaching them to obey everything I have commanded you."

Notice that this command is given by Christ to the Twelve under what we have seen in an earlier chapter is the dispensation of Law. So we must determine whether these instructions are vertical or horizontal. If they are horizontal then we should be practicing water baptism today in obedience to this command. But this passage gives an indication that Christ is here giving them instructions which are vertical and therefore not binding on us.

Three separate commands are given within the Great Commission. The first is to make disciples of all nations. Remember, Gentile salvation is not the mystery revealed to Paul. That Gentiles would be saved was prophesied many times in the Old Testament, but it was to happen through the agency of

Israel (see Zech. 8:23). The secret revealed to Paul is that Jew and Gentile are now equal before God with no preference given to Israel. Yet here in Matthew we have the twelve apostles, all Jews, sent out to evangelize.

After the command to baptize their converts the Twelve are told to teach them "to obey everything I have commanded you." That is, the apostles are to perpetuate the teaching they have received from Christ. To illustrate the vertical nature of this command consider what Christ taught the Twelve in Matthew 23:2,3. He said, "The teachers of the law and the Pharisees sit in Moses' seat. So you must obey them and do everything they tell you. But do not do what they do, for they do not practice what they preach." What kinds of things were the Pharisees teaching which the disciples were to obey? They were teaching conformity to the Mosaic Law, including all of the rituals, holy days, and ceremonies. Certainly the dietary laws, circumcision, and strict Sabbath observance were a part of this teaching. The disciples are to obey it all and, as we read in the Great Commission, teach others to obey it too.

If the portion of the Great Commission which commands water baptism is binding on us today then so also is the command to perpetuate everything Christ instructed for the disciples, including obedience to the Pharisees as they teach the Mosaic Law. Either that or it is best to view the command to water baptize as a vertical instruction given under the dispensation of Law when the Jewish ritual system was still in effect.

The third passage typically used as a basis for practicing water baptism today is Acts 2:38 where Peter instructed the believers to be baptized. We will take a closer look at the book of Acts in our next chapter, but a few things can be mentioned now which will help us understand Peter's instructions. Remember that what takes place here in Acts 2 is a continuation of God's agenda for Israel. Peter is offering the nation the kingdom which was promised through the prophets. Everything about this section of Acts is Jewish and consistent with God's relationship with Israel as His special people. So it is not surprising to find Jewish ceremonies being practiced.

Peter is here carrying out the commands given in the Great Commission. Just prior to His ascension Christ told the apostles they would be "witnesses in Jerusalem, and in all Judea and Samaria, and to the ends of the earth" (Acts 1:8). Notice that the message is to spread outward to the Gentiles from Jerusalem, an evidence of the Jewish priority. With the message that Jesus is the Messiah comes the ceremonies which are part of Israel's worship system.

TO BAPTIZE OR NOT TO BAPTIZE

I have never been baptized with water. When I tell people that, many of them are very surprised. "You have never been baptized?" No, that is not what I said. I said I have never been *water* baptized. I have been baptized by the Holy Spirit into the Body of Christ, and that produced a complete and permanent change in me. Paul says there is only one baptism for today, and I am thankful the baptism into His Body is the one I have received. I see no biblical basis in this dispensation of Grace for undergoing a Jewish ceremony which has its roots in the Mosaic Law.

Most Christians have had both the baptism into the Body of Christ and a water baptism. Is the latter something of no consequence, is it something for which they should ask forgiveness, or is it somewhere in between? The answer depends on what significance was attached to their water baptism.

A very few groups make water baptism a necessary part of the salvation experience. If you are not baptized in water, they say you are not truly saved. These groups also typically specify the method for that baptism, and if it was not done in exactly the manner they use, you are not saved. This is in clear contradiction to the message of the gospel which teaches us we are saved by faith apart from anything we do (Eph. 2:8,9; Titus 3:5).

Some denominations and churches make water baptism a requirement for membership. Their thinking is that because Christ required it of His followers anyone who has not been baptized in water is not walking in obedience and should therefore not be a member of their local assembly. These people would be quick to add that water baptism is not a requirement for salvation but is only an outward action which serves as a testimony to an inward reality.

As we have seen, Christ did command his followers to practice water baptism, but that command was given within the dispensation of Law and at a time when God was still dealing with Israel as His special people. To make the Jewish ceremony of water baptism a criterion for full participation in a local church is no different than those in Paul's day making the ceremony of circumcision or Sabbath observance a criterion. It puts a form of legalism into our fellowship that artificially creates classes within the church.

But perhaps the majority of Christians and denominations view water baptism as a voluntary act which is not required for either salvation or church membership. It is simply an act which bears witness to others of the new convert's faith in Christ. Many Christians look back on their water baptism as a significant event in their early days as a believer, maybe as the first time they made a public profession of faith. To be critical of such a motive and experience can seem almost like something more fitting of a theological Scrooge than a brother or sister in Christ.

I have no desire to call to repentance those who have been water baptized as though they have committed some great sin, nor to get out some ceremonial towel and dry them off. But I also would not encourage a new convert to go through the ceremony. First, it has no biblical basis in this dispensation, and our goal is to be as consistent as possible in obeying God's Word. Secondly, by going through the ceremony of water baptism a Christian may unwittingly contribute to the confusion about salvation that seems to be so common.

It is human nature to attach too much significance to outward ceremonies and not enough to real truth. To illustrate, let us suppose we agree all

Christians should wear orange on Thursdays. We will wear orange shirts, orange dresses, even orange shoes. When people ask us why we are dressed rather strangely we can tell them we do so in order to bear witness that we are different—we are children of God through faith in Christ. We are not Christians because we wear orange; we wear orange because we are Christians.

The practice of wearing orange on Thursdays seems a rather odd way of calling attention to our salvation, but then some might suggest that being immersed in water is also odd. But more than the oddity of it all is the real problem it will inevitably create. No matter how much we stress the fact that wearing orange does not make us Christians, human nature is such that some people will come to that conclusion anyway. As surely as the earth turns on its axis someone will say, "I want to be a Christian, and all the Christians I know wear orange on Thursdays. Therefore I will wear orange on Thursdays so I can be a Christian."

If you have talked to even a small sampling of people about their salvation you have undoubtedly heard some say they had the assurance of salvation because they were baptized in the church. With a few exceptions they probably heard the same thing you did—water baptism is a testimony of salvation not the means of receiving it. But human nature being what it is, and the Enemy being who he is, it is sure to happen that people will confuse the two. This confusion comes as a result of a practice, a ceremony, which is not part of God's instructions for the dispensation of Grace. The issue of salvation is a matter of heaven and hell, and we should do everything possible to avoid blurring the truth of God's grace.

It is a worthwhile effort to encourage a new Christian to make a public profession of faith. But instead of using an outdated Jewish ritual in a way God never intended and risking the confusion which too often accompanies it, we are better off to use a method which is both biblical and low risk. The verbal testimony backed up by a changed life is the most powerful witness available. Our friends the Thessalonian Christians were commended by Paul for just this testimony.

> The Lord's message rang out from you not only in Macedonia and Achaia—your faith in God has become known everywhere. Therefore we do not need to say anything about it, for they themselves report what kind of reception you gave us. They tell how you turned to God from idols to serve the living and true God (1 Thess. 1:8,9).

It was undoubtedly this readiness to tell others and their transformed lives which made them susceptible to persecution. Everyone knew who the Christians were in Thessalonica.

Water baptism is an issue which has caused serious division in the church throughout her history. In the decades following the Protestant Reformation many were put to death because their refusal to baptize infants was seen as a serious heresy. That kind of reaction certainly elevates the matter to a level far higher than it deserves. Those who do not place any value in water baptism for salvation but see it merely as a means of making a public profession of faith are brothers and sisters in Christ. Their practice of the ceremony may be seen by them as a basis for being a Christian in good standing with God and the church, and that comes dangerously close to the legalism Scripture denounces. If, however, it is what we have described as most common, a means of profession, it comes from a motive we respect, even admire. We encourage these fellow believers to take another look at the Bible and what it says on the topic of water baptism. Nothing reduces risk and brings blessing like being thoroughly biblical.

STUDY QUESTIONS

1. What is the meaning of the word *baptism*?
2. Where does our English word *baptism* come from, and why is it not found in the Old Testament?
3. What is the origin of the ceremony of water baptism?
4. What was the function of water baptism?
5. What is the meaning of the baptism Paul describes in Romans 6?
6. What baptism does Paul say is the only one which is functioning today?
7. Identify one of the passages used to support the continuing practice of water baptism and explain why it does not.
8. What is the practical risk associated with water baptism?

- Chapter 10 -

THE TRANSITION PERIOD

A unique time in history

Early in married life my masculine instincts got the better of me and I decided I needed to build something. What I would build was not as important as the fact I would build it, which helps explain why I settled on a clothes hamper as my first project. I probably could have purchased two nice hampers for the money I spent on materials, but this was about being a male, not about being sensible. Several days and a sore thumb later I was the proud owner of the world's only forty-pound clothes hamper. What it lacked in beauty it more than made up for in sturdiness!

Unfortunately, I neglected to measure the bathroom door before I began this project, which meant my piece of artistry had to sit in the living room of our very small apartment. For reasons I will never understand, my wife decided this did *not* fit the decor, and so the hamper ended up as a storage bin off the back porch.

I see a similarity between my forty-pound hamper and theology. No matter how artfully a theology is presented or how solid it seems, if it is not consistent when compared with the pages of Scripture it is not good theology. It may look good right up until the bathroom door, but that is not enough. It has to fit through the door.

A MATTER OF CHRONOLOGY

We have seen how God has dealt with humankind through a series of dispensations. We learned that this present dispensation was a mystery revealed to the apostle Paul, and that Jew and Gentile are now equal before God. Along with this temporary setting aside of Israel as God's special people, the various methodologies God used to deal with Israel have also been set aside. These include indirect miracles and outward ceremonies such as water baptism. Also, the Body of Christ has been given a future which is distinct from the agenda God laid out for Israel.

It is at this point a serious flaw seems to appear. If miraculous signs and water baptism were discontinued with the beginning of the dispensation of Grace, how come the book of Acts records many examples of Paul doing both? He heals the sick, raises the dead, and baptizes converts. Paul is the one to whom the revelation of the mystery was given. We would expect if these elements are not part of this dispensation then Paul would be the last person to use them in his ministry. But the record in Acts indicates just the opposite. Does this suggest baptism and indirect miracles should have a part in this dispensation after all? Does our dispensational interpretation fail at the bathroom door?

God is all-powerful and can do anything not inconsistent with His holiness. Accordingly, He may administer the dispensations and the changes between them any way He chooses. A careful study of Acts and the Epistles indicates God chose to bring about the change from the dispensation of Law to the dispensation of Grace through the process of a transition. The book of Acts, beginning at chapter 9 and Paul's conversion, records that transition.

This transition can be better understood if we know the sequence of events following Paul's conversion, including the order of the Pauline Epistles. Diagramed as a time line it would look like Figure 10.a.

Notice that the portion of Paul's ministry covered by the book of Acts includes his conversion, three missionary journeys, and his trip to Rome where he was imprisoned. These events cover the years from A.D. 35 to A.D. 62. During these twenty-eight years Paul wrote Galatians, 1 and 2 Thessalonians, 1 and 2 Corinthians, and Romans. At the point where the Acts narrative stops Paul was in prison awaiting trial. During this time he wrote Ephesians, Philippians, Colossians, and Philemon. He was eventually released, traveled more, and wrote 1 Timothy and Titus. He was then re-arrested and wrote 2 Timothy just before his martyrdom in Rome in A.D. 68.

The group of letters Paul wrote during his missionary journeys (the portion of his ministry recorded in Acts) is referred to as the Pre-prison Epistles, while the term Prison Epistles refers to the four letters (Eph., Phil., Col., Phile.) written during his first Roman imprisonment. The books of

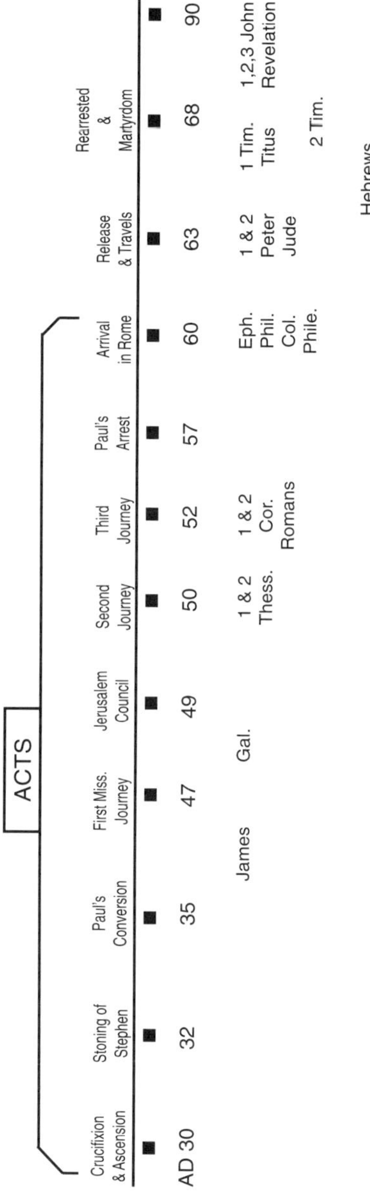
ACTS
Crucifixion & Ascension
AD 30
Stoning of Stephen
32
Paul's Conversion
35
James
First Miss. Journey
47
Gal.
Jerusalem Council
49
Second Journey
50
1 & 2 Thess.
Third Journey
52
1 & 2 Cor.
Romans
Paul's Arrest
57
Arrival in Rome
60
Eph.
Phil.
Col.
Phile.
Release & Travels
63
1 & 2 Peter
Jude
Hebrews
Rearrested & Martyrdom
68
1 Tim.
Titus
2 Tim.
90
1,2,3 John
Revelation

Figure 10.a

1 and 2 Timothy and Titus are known as the Pastoral Epistles because those two men were pastors.

This chronology is important because of the difference we notice when we compare the Acts narrative and the Epistles written during that time with the Prison and Pastoral Epistles written after the close of the book of Acts. We can see a transition, a shift, from a methodology which includes some of the elements of the Jewish program to a ministry in which they are completely absent.

In Acts 14:8-10 we read that Paul healed a man lame from birth. In Acts 16 he cast a spirit out of a slave girl, and Acts 19:11,12 says, "God did extraordinary miracles through Paul. Handkerchiefs and aprons that had touched him were taken to the sick, and their illnesses were cured and the evil spirits left them." Chapter 20 records the incident involving Eutychus who fell from a third floor window but was raised from the dead by Paul.

Contrast this sampling from Acts with the record of the Prison and Pastoral Epistles. In Philippians 2:25-30 Paul tells them of Epaphroditus, Paul's fellow worker, who almost died because of an illness while with Paul. He counsels Timothy to "stop drinking only water, and use a little wine because of your stomach and your frequent illnesses" (1 Tim. 5:23). In 2 Timothy 4:20 Paul writes "I left Trophimus sick in Miletus." Why are these men, close associates of Paul, left to struggle and nearly die with physical ailments while earlier Paul healed people he had never met?

ISRAEL'S NEED FOR AUTHENTICATION

Remember that Israel had, for almost 1,500 years, been God's special people and the objects of His grace. Any blessings God bestowed He gave to Israel because they were His favored nation. They came to think of themselves in that way and a significant amount of spiritual pride settled in. It was because of this arrogance that John the Baptist warned them, "Do not think you can say to yourselves, 'We have Abraham as our father.' I tell you that out of these stones God can raise up children from Abraham" (Matt. 3:9). This spiritual conceit undoubtedly had a lot to do with their refusal to accept the notion they had crucified their Messiah.

Imagine the reaction of the Jews when Paul came to them and announced they had been set aside by God who was now extending His grace to the Gentiles on an equal basis! The very idea of it was near blasphemy, and in many cases their reaction was violence toward Paul. They were certainly not going to accept such heresy just because a Christian zealot said so, even if he had been a Pharisee.

God could have let their rejection stand as it was and proceeded with the new order. However, in His grace God indulged the Jews by establishing the authenticity of Paul's message in a way suited to the Jewish temperament—He accredited it with signs (*saemeion*).

We see this frequently because during the early portion of Paul's ministry it was his pattern when he entered a new city to go first to the synagogue. This was primarily for practical not theological reasons. The content of his message was that Jesus is the Savior for both Jew and Gentile without distinction. But the synagogue contained a group that, unlike the Gentile population around them, believed in one God and accepted the authority of what we now call the Old Testament. This made them a receptive audience, at least in theory. So Paul would go to the synagogues and preach the gospel, including its universal application to Jew and Gentile. However, as a concession to Jewish skepticism God accredited Paul's message through the means of indirect miracles.

A good example of this dynamic is Paul's ministry in the city of Corinth. Acts 18 tells us about the founding of the Corinthian church on Paul's second missionary journey. Here we read that Paul began his ministry as usual in the synagogue, but when the Jews rejected his message he left saying, "Your blood be on your own heads! I am clear of my responsibility. From now on I will go to the Gentiles" (v. 6). The church which he then founded met right next door to the synagogue at the house of Titius Justus, a Gentile. Surprisingly, one of the earliest converts was Crispus, the synagogue ruler. The Jews replaced Crispus with Sosthenes, who himself eventually became a Christian (see 1 Cor. 1:1). In other words, the founding of the church in Corinth early in Paul's ministry was done in a setting which included strong Jewish roots. This fits well with what Paul later writes to them in 2 Corinthians 12:12: "The things that mark an apostle—signs, wonders, and miracles—were done among you with great perseverance."

ISRAEL'S NEED ACCOMMODATED

Paul received a revelation from God that Israel was being set aside and the gospel was to go to the Gentiles without distinction. He preached this universal gospel everywhere he went, including the synagogues. But the Jews require signs (1 Cor. 1:22) and so were not inclined to believe Paul's message was from God, especially because it violated their sense of being unique in God's sight. Therefore, even though He had set them aside, God in His grace temporarily accredited Paul's message with the miraculous signs which the Jews demand (see Rom. 15:18,19). These miracles characterized the early part of Paul's ministry, as recorded in Acts and the Epistles written during this time period. But when Paul had traversed the Roman empire, preaching the gospel from Jerusalem to Rome, God withdrew the sign methodology because the validity of Paul's message had been clearly established. The message had been proclaimed, the Jews' need for signs had been accommodated, and their continued rejection would indeed be upon their own heads.

We have local examples of this in the book of Acts as three times Paul tells a Jewish audience their rejection of his gospel leads him to the Gentiles. In Antioch of Pisidia (Acts 13:46), Corinth (Acts 18:6), and finally in Rome (Acts 28:28) Paul announces his plan to leave the Jews to their disbelief and turn to the Gentiles. Notice the geographical progression of these three pronouncements as Paul moves from east to west across the empire.

Of all Paul's teaching for the Body of Christ contained in his Epistles, only one, 1 Corinthians, discusses what we have called indirect miracles. Chapters 12 through 14 of this early book have as their topic "spiritual gifts" (12:1), and within this section Paul makes reference to miraculous powers, healing, tongues, and the interpretation of tongues. These latter two receive more attention from Paul apparently because they had been misused in the Corinthian church. Whole books have been written on this portion of Scripture, and as you might guess, interpretations vary greatly. But one thing seems to be indisputable—Paul downplays the role of tongues in the church. He goes so far as to tell the Corinthians that, "Where there are tongues, they will be stilled" (13:8). He thus prepares them for the time when God will withdraw the indirect miracle as a means of accrediting the message of Gentile equality.

In the Prison and Pastoral Epistles no mention is made of anything associated with indirect miracles. This is especially significant because in the Pastorals Paul wrote to two men who were in positions of leadership about how the local church should carry out its mission (see 1 Tim. 3:14,15). Instead, these later letters of Paul, written after the close of Acts, describe situations in which the miracle of healing would have been especially appropriate but was not used.

PAUL'S PRACTICE OF WATER BAPTISM

What we have said explains why Paul performed miracles during the early portion of his ministry but it does not answer the question about his use of water baptism. This Jewish ritual did not serve as a means of authentication, validating Paul's message. Why, then, did he baptize any converts at all? The answer emerges when we look at those passages which talk about Paul and his use of water baptism.

It surprises some to discover there are, at the most, only four places in Acts where Paul baptizes. In chapter 16 Paul baptizes Lydia, a Jewish convert, and her household. Later in the same chapter he baptizes the Philippian jailer and his household. In chapter 18 Paul baptizes converts at Corinth and in chapter 19 he *may* have baptized a group of disciples who had been followers of John the Baptist.

The reason we hesitate to say Paul did baptize the group in Acts 19 is because there is a question about how to place the punctuation in the passage. First-century Greek did not have the punctuation marks we have in English; the readers of that time depended on context to tell them things we know from periods, commas, and quotation marks. So when our English versions put in these marks we need to understand the translators are making a judgment about where they should go. Generally the context makes it clear, but occasionally it is difficult to determine, and Acts 19:4,5 is one of these difficult cases. The passage as it reads in the NIV is punctuated as follows:

> Paul said, "John's baptism was a baptism of repentance. He told the people to believe in the one coming after him, that is, in Jesus." On hearing this, they were baptized into the name of the Lord Jesus.

Some think the quotation marks which indicate Paul is speaking should be placed after the last sentence, which is verse 5 in the text. If this is the case, "they" of verse 5 refers to the people John baptized instead of the verse telling us Paul baptized these disciples. Other grammatical features of the two verses seem to support this conclusion.

So we have at most four, and perhaps only three, cases in Acts of Paul using water baptism. This is certainly a contrast to the large role the practice of water baptism had in the early chapters of Acts. Despite the fact Paul's ministry was at least as evangelistic as Peter's, Paul does not include water baptism as a part of the conversion process (contrast Acts 2:38 with 16:31). This illustrates again what we saw in our last chapter—Paul's ministry and the gospel which he preached did not involve Jewish ceremonies, including water baptism.

In 1 Corinthians 1:14-17 we are given an explanation for both the move away from baptism as a part of the conversion experience and Paul's rare usage of it. Remember that 1 Corinthians is one of Paul's early letters and that it was written to a city which is one of the three or four settings in Acts where Paul did use water baptism.

In this section of 1 Corinthians Paul discusses the problem of divisions in the Corinthian church. The believers had broken up into little cliques, each claiming loyalty to a particular leader. In response to this problem Paul says,

> I am thankful that I did not baptize any of you except Crispus and Gaius, so no one can say that you were baptized into my name. (Yes, I also baptized the household of Stephanas; beyond that, I don't remember if I baptized anyone else.) For Christ did not send me to baptize, but to preach

> the gospel—not with words of human wisdom, lest the cross of Christ be emptied of its power.

Paul here downplays the role of baptism in his ministry. In Matthew 28:19 Christ commanded the Twelve to go out and evangelize, "baptizing them in the name of the Father and of the Son and of the Holy Spirit." But Paul says he is thankful he did not baptize but a few of the Corinthian Christians. This contrast shows us again how different Paul's ministry was from that of the Twelve; he was not operating under the same instructions they were. The apostles were commanded to baptize their converts and Paul is glad he did not. Water baptism was not a part of Paul's commission.

Then why do we have in Acts even these few examples of Paul using the ceremony? The answer once again is the transition period which the book of Acts records. The three or four examples are all early in his ministry—the last recorded case of Paul using water baptism is during his second missionary journey—and in each case the environment is especially Jewish. Lydia, in chapter 16, was part of a group of Jewish women meeting on the Sabbath outside of town. Both cases in chapter 18 are in the city where the church started in the synagogue and then moved right next door. The Ephesian disciples (if they were baptized by Paul) were Jews who had been followers of John.

Early in his ministry, during a period of transition, Paul used both indirect miracles and Jewish ritual because of their effectiveness in communicating to the Jewish community the change God had made. But by the third missionary journey (the period of time when 1 Corinthians was written) Paul is already saying he is glad he had baptized very few of them. This statement is not, as some have suggested, simply Paul saying he is glad someone else did the baptizing so they could not claim any special attachment to him. His statement, "Christ did not send me to baptize, but to preach the gospel" (v.17) is a declaration about what should and should not be done, not who should do it. God has decreed one baptism for this dispensation (Eph. 4:5) and it is the baptism by which the Holy Spirit places us into the Body of Christ (1 Cor. 12:13).

ANOTHER TRANSITION ISSUE

God chose to use a period of transition to establish the authenticity of Paul's message to the Jews that they had been set aside. This transition was one of methodology and had concluded by the end of the book of Acts. A diagram of the shift would look something like this:

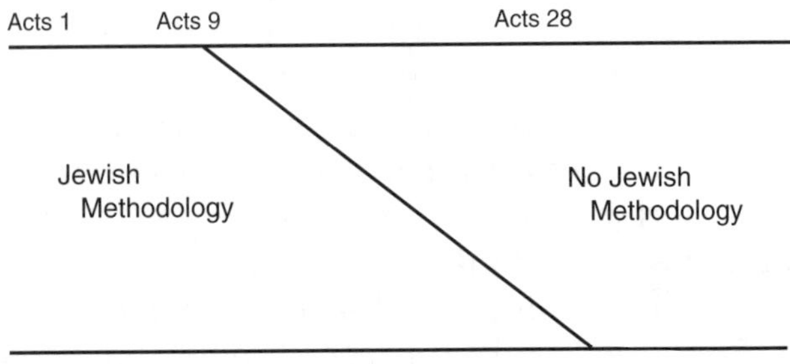

Figure 10.b

Miraculous signs and Jewish ceremonies were merely means through which God communicated to Israel. But what about the message itself? Did God change the dispensational arrangement abruptly, moving from the dispensation of Law to the dispensation of Grace at one point in time? Or did He gradually phase out the former dispensation as He simultaneously phased in the present one? Was there a transition of message as well as methodology?

This question focuses on believers who were saved before and remained alive after Paul received the revelation of this current dispensation. For example, a sizeable group of Jews believed and were saved on the day of Pentecost in Acts 2. The nation of Israel went on to reject the offer of the Kingdom, but those individuals certainly remained saved. Did God begin the dispensation of Grace abruptly, and transfer into the Body of Christ those who were already saved? Or did God leave those pre-Pauline believers under the terms and conditions of the dispensation of Law and only place in the Body of Christ those who were saved after the mystery was revealed to Paul? These two options, when diagramed, look like Figure 10.c.

The top diagram represents the view which understands God to have continued the dispensation of Law until any believers prior to Paul's revelation had died. These pre-Pauline believers are represented by the "X" on the diagram. The bottom diagram illustrates the opinion that God changed dispensations abruptly and any believers who were alive when Paul received his revelation of the mystery were transferred into the Body of Christ.

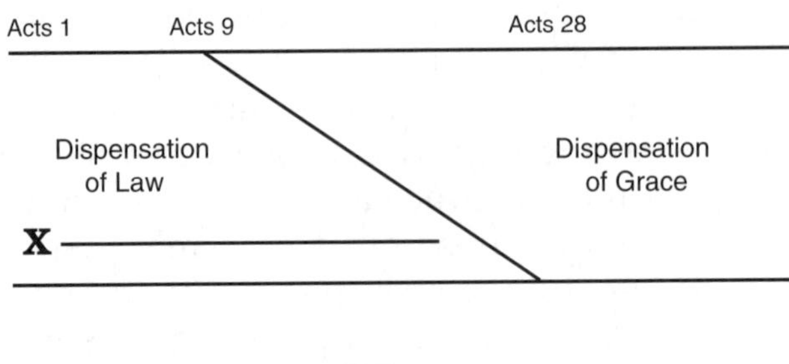

OR...

Acts 1 Acts 9 Acts 28

Dispensation of Law

Dispensation of Grace

X

Figure 10.c

This might seem like a very insignificant issue at first, but it has one important ramification. Peter, James, and John (as well as the whole group of apostles) were among the group of pre-Pauline believers. Their point of personal salvation was earlier than Pentecost, but they also lived beyond the beginning of this dispensation. Because these three men wrote books of the New Testament, their dispensational position is important.

Take Peter as an example. If God continued the dispensation of Law until all pre-Pauline believers had died (the top portion of the diagram), then Peter, a member of that group, wrote his epistles to Jews within that dispensational setting. Therefore, his letters need to be read with the same care as the Old Testament books, with attention to vertical and horizontal truths. On the other hand, if God made the change abruptly and Peter became a member of the Body of Christ, then anything he wrote after that point (i.e. both 1 and 2 Peter) is completely applicable to the Body of Christ. He may have written to Jews, but they were still members of the Body of Christ.

This issue has been vigorously debated and evidence has been cited to support both views. The discussion has sometimes made the whole thing seem far too complex for the average person to grasp. Fortunately, we have a resolution which does not answer the question directly but greatly reduces its significance.

When we read the New Testament epistles written by pre-Pauline believers we discover that almost all of what they have to say is clearly horizontal in nature and applies equally well to God's people in any dispensation. When James warns about the dangers of the tongue, or Peter talks about suffering for Christ, or John speaks about loving in word and deed, I can and should apply it to my life.

In a few of these books, generally called the Jewish Christian Epistles, some passages will be interpreted differently depending on the view one takes. Those who believe God continued the dispensation of Law until pre-Pauline believers died, understand these passages to teach vertical truth directed exclusively to Israel under that dispensation. Those who believe pre-Pauline believers were transferred into the Body of Christ interpret the same passages as teaching truth which applies to us today. These latter interpreters say the only reason Jewish terminology is used is because the readers were raised in Judaism and related best to that kind of language.

CONCLUSION

The study of the book of Acts can be very profitable. The book opens with a focus on Peter and a ministry to Israel as the nation is presented with an offer of the Kingdom. By the end of Acts the action has shifted to Rome, the Gentiles are the audience, and the Body of Christ is the center of God's work. Without Acts we would have no historical framework for understanding what Paul teaches in his letters. How can it be that the Gospels are so thoroughly Jewish and yet Paul writes that God does not distinguish between Jews and Gentiles? The book of Acts gives us the answer as it describes Paul's role as the one to whom God gave the revelation of the mystery.

This dispensational change may have been brought about by God gradually or abruptly. In either case a transition in methodology exists, and Paul's later epistles describe the guidelines which should govern the Body of Christ until He comes.

STUDY QUESTIONS

1. Name the Pauline Epistles which were written during the period of time covered in the book of Acts.
2. Explain why Paul performed indirect miracles during the early portion of his ministry.
3. How many times in the book of Acts does Paul baptize new believers?
4. Why did Paul baptize at all?
5. What does Paul say about water baptism in 1 Corinthians?
6. Explain the two views about the change from the dispensation of Law to the dispensation of Grace.
7. What significance does this issue have for Bible study?

- Chapter 11 -

DISPENSATIONALISM AS A SYSTEM

A look at the whole

In the preceding chapters we have outlined a very basic overview of dispensationalism. We have looked at its foundation—the literal or normal interpretation of Scripture. With a literal hermeneutic we were led to the conclusion God has dealt with humankind in different ways at different times. Paul uses the term *oikonomia*, or dispensation, to describe these varying relationships. Having come to an understanding of that concept through the use of the word in Luke 16 we saw how human history has indeed been a series of dispensations with some horizontal and some vertical truths.

With this as a base we focused on the current *oikonomia*, the dispensation of Grace, and noted its essential features, including when it began and God's will for His people in this age. The result is a picture of individual and church life which does not include some of the features of God's relationship with Israel under the dispensation of Law.

At this point it is possible and helpful to step back and look at the whole of dispensationalism. What are the advantages of dispensationalism?

What are some of the criticisms which have been made about the system and are they valid? What role does dispensationalism play in living the Christian life? Does it contribute to our goal to do the will of God or is it a dry theological system with no practical value other than as a topic for academic discussions?

THE BENEFITS OF DISPENSATIONALISM

In 1384 the first English version of the Bible was published under the direction of John Wycliffe. Until that time the Roman Catholic Church, believing only the clergy could be trusted with the Word of God, had restricted publication of Scripture to Latin versions. Wycliffe believed God gave the Bible to all the people, and that the people should be able to read it themselves. Not surprisingly, his efforts to put the Bible back in the hands of the common person got him in a lot of trouble with the church at Rome. But the hold which the Roman church had on the Scriptures was broken, and later Martin Luther (in 1522) and William Tyndale (in 1525) also translated the Bible into the everyday language of the people.

Today we have a number of different English translations available to us. But many Christians are still afraid of the Bible, convinced only trained professionals are capable of understanding its deep and complex meanings. As in the days before Wycliffe, they leave it once again to the clergy to tell them what the Bible says and what it means.

One of the greatest benefits of dispensationalism is that it understands what the Bible says to be the same thing as what it means. The literal hermeneutic does theologically what Wycliffe did linguistically—it puts the Bible in the hands of the people. There is no need for the sophisticated allegorical interpretations of covenant theology which require a prior knowledge of spiritual truth. Apart from figures of speech, most of which are fairly obvious, what a person reads in the Bible is what God means. As a result, the average Christian is fully capable of understanding Scripture.

Dispensationalism also opens the Bible to the ordinary Christian by answering the dilemma of contradictions within Scripture. One reason some Christians are sure the Bible has complex meanings known only to the clergy is that they read passages which contradict each other. Because most Christians believe the Bible to be without error they take these contradictions to prove special interpretive skill is required in order to resolve these conflicts.

Dispensationalism explains that what is too often thought to be a contradiction is really just God dealing with humankind in different ways at different times. The specific requirements of a particular dispensation may be quite different from those of a dispensation which preceded it. The Bible does not contain contradictions; it records God's changing requirements through a series of dispensations. Once this is understood most of the troublesome contradictions disappear.

A literal hermeneutic and a dispensational approach to Scripture allow the ordinary Christian to read his or her Bible and comprehend it. God did give the Body of Christ pastors and teachers who have additional training and skill to help us understand Scripture's complex truths. However, it is the Word of God and no scholar will ever fully grasp its content. We need and are thankful for those whom God has gifted in teaching us the Bible. But all of us can read the Bible for ourselves, and because Scripture means what it says we can understand and grow as we read.

This combination of a literal hermeneutic and a dispensational perspective will also help us avoid some of the errors which, in the extreme, can be very dangerous. If vertical commands from another dispensation are made requirements for this age the result can be rigid legalism. Paul encountered this when some Jews in the early church sought to put Christians back under the requirements of the Mosaic Law. This dangerous trend is the basis for much of what Paul says in Galatians and Colossians.

An example of this same dynamic is the growing movement within contemporary Christianity which has as its goal the restructuring of the American legal system in order to bring it into compliance with the Mosaic Law. This effort, known as theonomy or reconstructionism sounds like a good idea at first. After all, the Mosaic Law represented God's design for a just society. But it fails to recognize God had a unique relationship with Israel within the dispensation of Law. The civil portion of the Law was designed for an agricultural society living in a land promised to them by God. Furthermore, the basis for Israel's government was the concept of *theocracy* in which church and state are the same. Thus, the logic of reconstructionism eventually disposes of democracy, because it believes God has directly determined through the Mosaic Law how society should structure itself. This view is inconsistent with Paul's command that we obey those in authority over us whether or not they are Christians (Rom. 13:1-7). Nowhere does Paul say anything which supports the notion we should return to a civil government like Israel's. A dispensational approach to Scripture will keep us from this kind of error.

The mistake of reconstructionism is trying to bring the requirements of one dispensation directly and fully into the present, without regard for God's changing relationship with humankind. At the other extreme is the danger of allegorizing Scripture to the extent that any passage can be made to say anything. For example, a Gentile country in Scripture is interpreted to represent America's current enemy, or a prophetic passage is made to speak directly about some present-day event. Those who abandon their own careful study of the Bible and accept the allegorical interpretations of another individual may find themselves being led into some very dangerous territory.

Accurate dispensationalism also provides guidance in the midst of a baffling variety of perspectives on Christian life and worship. One group baptizes by immersion, another by sprinkling. This church believes in speaking in tongues and healings while that one does not. One Christian says tithing is God's standard of giving while another insists we should give at whatever level we think is appropriate for us. No wonder many people give up trying to find an objective standard for all Christians and take the position believers should decide for themselves what God wants for them. "What is right for one Christian may not be right for another."

If speaking in tongues is God's will for one congregation, it is right for all congregations. It is either a part of God's plan for this age or it is not. We cannot have it both ways, even if our motive is to preserve harmony within the Body. Unity at the expense of truth is a hazardous course. So which configuration of all the options for the Christian life does the Bible teach?

Only a dispensational understanding of the Bible can provide the answer. Distinguishing between God's directives to His people in the different dispensations will show us what He wants of His people today. We will never agree on all the details of the Bible. Again, it is the Word of God and therefore reflects His infiniteness. But surely God wants His people to know His will for them individually and as a church. Dispensationalism provides the means for discovering that will and its uniqueness as compared to God's will in other ages.

CRITICISMS OF DISPENSATIONALISM

Like any theological system, dispensationalism has its critics. Criticism can be helpful, as it is when it causes us to look more carefully at what we say and make corrections where necessary. But criticism can also be unfair when it is based on inaccurate statements or faulty logic.

Dispensationalism will continue to be refined and its critics will help that process along. However, much of the negative commentary about dispensational theology is either not factual or not valid. A brief survey of the more common charges should prove helpful.

Some who reject dispensationalism say the system is a recent development, and therefore not part of the historical belief of the church. They argue that the early church fathers did not teach anything like dispensational theology, but instead saw the Bible as a unified whole. The reformers, like Luther and Calvin, also never proposed anything which resembles modern-day dispensationalism. These critics contend the system first appeared in the writings of John Nelson Darby in the mid-1800s. No theology which first appears eighteen centuries into the church's existence can possibly be valid. Dispensational theology, the critics say, is a recent error out of harmony with the historical beliefs of the church.

This charge contains some measure of truth. The early church fathers did not write about dispensationalism in the same way recent theologians have. Nor did they write about a lot of things which are important to recent scholars, and for a very good reason. The church in the first few centuries had its hands full defining the basic doctrines which form the foundations of Christianity. Those great men were occupied with setting forth important doctrines like the deity of Christ, redemption through His blood, and the Personhood of the Holy Spirit. This was urgent in the face of heretics who challenged these very fundamental truths. The writings of the early church do not contain a developed dispensational theology because the pressing need of the time was for a clear presentation of the foundational doctrines of the faith.

Many church fathers did, however, write things which contain the basic ideas of dispensationalism in elementary form. Justin Martyr (A.D. 110-165), Irenaeus (A.D. 130-200), and Clement of Alexandria (A.D. 150-220) each made reference in their writings to the different ways God dealt with humankind in different periods of history. These and other examples can be cited which show that the concepts of dispensational theology, though not developed in the writings of the early church, are consistent with what the church fathers said.

John Nelson Darby was one of the first to present a developed and systematic dispensationalism. The period between the church fathers and Darby was occupied by the Dark Ages during which the Roman Catholic Church defined truth, and then by the Reformation which was a time devoted to recovering the basic doctrines of salvation. By the 1800s the church was turning its attention to the relationship between church and state and to eschatology. Both of these issues are closely related to dispensationalism, which explains why Darby and others of his time wrote extensively about dispensational theology.

Developed dispensationalism is not present in the writings of the church fathers, but the basic concepts do appear. The theology is more fully set forth beginning in the 1800s because of the natural progression of concerns in Christianity. The historic faith of the church serves as a guide against error, and we should approach with caution anything which deviates from that tradition. But the church fathers did not speak with infallibility, nor did they address every area of biblical truth. The final authority on the validity of dispensational theology should be the Word of God. If the system is biblical it is correct.

A second accusation brought against dispensational theology is that it throws out much of the Bible, declaring it to be irrelevant to Christians today. Two factors have led to this criticism. Unfortunately, some dispensationalists, in their zeal to emphasize the differences between God's administrations, have neglected the important horizontal truths of Scripture. These individuals would never actually say the Old Testament has no value to New Testament Christians, but their sermons and writings sometimes give that impression. However, on occasion covenant theology has falsely characterized the majority of dispensationalists who have been balanced in their approach to Scripture. All Scripture is God-breathed and deserves our careful attention.

This accusation of ignoring whole sections of the Bible has also been made by some dispensationalists against other dispensationalists. The most common form of dispensational theology begins the present dispensation in Acts 2 at Pentecost. This was the view of C. I. Scofield, a Dallas pastor and Bible conference speaker who published the Scofield Reference Bible in 1909. The tremendous popularity of this Bible and its helpful notes have been a key factor in the spread of both dispensationalism and Scofield's view of an Acts 2 beginning for the Body of Christ. We have taken the position in this book that the dispensation of Grace and the Body of Christ began with the ministry of the apostle Paul and the revelation of the mystery given to him. This view is much less common, but as we saw with the charge of dispensationalism as a recent development, the real question is not popularity but biblical accuracy.

The mid-Acts view of the beginning of this dispensation understands Paul to be the one through whom God revealed His will for the Body of Christ. Therefore, his epistles have particular relevance for Christians today. Because this is a more narrow perspective than an early-Acts position, it is even more susceptible to the charge of tossing out most of the Bible. Often the frightening term *ultradispensationalist* has been used by Acts 2 dispensationalists of those who take a mid-Acts position, giving the impression they belong to some extremist cult. Perhaps a few who hold a mid-Acts view have contributed to this perception by overstating the unique elements of the Pauline revelation or by using a rather harsh tone.

Hopefully the preceding chapters of this book have made it clear that no thoughtful dispensationalist, regardless of when he or she begins the present dispensation, would disregard any portion of God's Word. It is necessary to distinguish between the portions written directly to the Body of Christ and those addressed to other dispensations. But horizontal truths are present throughout Scripture, and on each page of the Bible we can learn of God's nature and ways.

This brings us to the third common charge brought against dispensationalism. Some critics have said dispensationalism is divisive and has a history of splitting churches. This accusation is sometimes supported by the report of a particular situation in which a few zealous dispensationalists insisted on spreading their views in a church with a different heritage. This eventually led to a bitter church split and great harm to the work of God.

Again, this has undoubtedly happened on occasion. Good theology does not guarantee appropriate behavior, and dispensationalism is no exception. But it is also true that there comes a point when believers disagree about matters of significant doctrine to such an extent it is best for them to part company. When this happens it should be done in a way consistent with our relationship as brothers and sisters in Christ. To go our separate ways quietly and graciously in order to pursue what we earnestly believe to be the teachings of Scripture is a course of action with a strong historical precedent.

SO WHAT?

A good sermon or Sunday School lesson should always have a "So what?" It is not enough to preach or teach good solid doctrine based on sound biblical interpretation. We are obligated to show how that truth impacts life. Our listeners should never listen to sound doctrine and then leave asking, "So what?"

After all that has been said about dispensationalism, what value, if any, does it have for life? What should we do with what we know?

Dispensational theology makes the Bible understandable to the ordinary person. The literal hermeneutic and its answer to the apparent contradictions in Scripture mean it requires no special theological expertise to grasp the basic teachings of God's Word. Therefore, the most obvious response to dispensationalism is to become a regular reader of God's Word.

This is a difficult habit to cultivate in a time and culture like ours. The combined influences of the visual media and "instant everything" discourage the discipline of regular Bible reading. Instead, we hire experts, paying them to do the reading and studying for us so we can get just the essentials in a not-to-exceed-thirty-minutes message on Sunday.

Perhaps like me you can remember the sight of your grandmother sitting alone at the kitchen table early in the morning reading her Bible. Have we stopped doing that because life is too hectic, or is life too hectic because we have stopped doing that? The Word of God is the methodology He has chosen to make the Christian life productive in the fullest, most complete sense. "All Scripture is God-breathed and is useful . . . so that the man of God may be thoroughly equipped for every good work" (2 Tim. 3:16,17). We are fortunate to have gifted preachers and teachers who can teach us about effective living. But too many Christians have allowed these helps to become a replacement for their own regular Bible reading. Dispensationalists, more than anyone else, should be people of the Book. We are committed not only to its inspiration but also its accessibility to any who read it. *Lord, help us to be regular readers of Your Word.*

Dispensationalists should also be gracious people. It is ironic that those who understand the blessings which are ours through the opening of the gospel to everyone can on occasion be so ungracious toward others. Traditions so easily turn into legalism—standards by which we judge someone's orthodoxy. The spiritual inferiority of the Gentile gets replaced by the inferiority of the divorced, or the one who dresses in an unusual way.

Dispensationalists should have a deep appreciation for what it means to have been "separate from Christ, excluded from citizenship in Israel and foreigners to the covenants of the promise, without hope and without God in the world" (Eph. 2:12). But now, thanks to His grace, we have full access to God through Christ. There is no more basis for exclusion. His grace opens the way for all. If we believe this to be true then certainly above all people we must be gracious to others who are outcasts.

In Matthew 18:21-35 we read of the servant who had a very large debt graciously cancelled by his master. But this servant went out and had a fellow servant thrown in jail because of his inability to pay a debt of a few dollars. We must not be like that unmerciful servant. Having experienced the grace of God we must show grace to all, knowing it will never come close to what He has done for us.

Finally, dispensationalists should be joyful people. Yes, we struggle with the difficulties of life and grieve at the death of loved ones. But we do not grieve like those who have no hope (1 Thess. 4:13), and we know that "our present sufferings are not worth comparing with the glory that will be revealed in us" (Rom. 8:18).

No member of the Body of Christ needs to worry about the Tribulation because "God did not appoint us to suffer wrath but to receive salvation" (1 Thess. 5:9). Whether we die first or live until He comes in the air for the Body of Christ we have the assurance we will receive glorified resurrection bodies at the Rapture. This should produce within us a peace and joy which is deeper than the temporary trials of today.

STUDY QUESTIONS

1. Identify three benefits of dispensationalism.
2. What is the goal of *reconstructionism* and what is its flaw?
3. Identify and respond to three of the criticisms brought against dispensationalism.
4. What impact should dispensationalism have on the Christian life?